AF669065

EDUCATION: Planning and Human Development

EDUCATION
Planning and Human Development

(In 8 Volumes)

Literacy and Non-formal Education

(Volume 2)

V.C. PANDEY

ISHA BOOKS

DELHI—110 033

EDUCATION: Planning and Human Development
(Education)

Rs. 7000 (Set in 8 Vols.)

ISBN: 81-8205-006-5 (Set)
ISBN: 81-8205-008-1 (Vol. 2)

Published in 2003 in India by
Isha Books, D-43, Prithviraj Road
Adarsh Nagar, Delhi-110 033

Lasertypesetting by: Varsha Graphics, Delhi
Printed at: Chawla Offset Press, Delhi

Preface

In most countries, non-formal education was found highly effective not only in addressing the inadequacies of formal school in terms of retention and completion rates, adaptability and functionality but also in catering to the learning needs of different target groups, i. e., those children who cannot or do not get enrolled in primary school, those who drop out from school, youths and adults who relapse into illiteracy and those who have never benefited from any schooling.

As far as education remains in the heart of the poverty alleviation strategies, non-formal education appears to be particularly helpful in that it enables the rural or urban poor and other marginalized groups to acquire useful knowledge, attitudes and skills. Besides, non-formal education affords wide array of learning opportunities directly associated with income driven activities. Therefore, non-formal education programmes play an important complementary and supplementary role to attaining the EFA goals. Today, most of experts as well as EFA partners agencies are convinced that it is impossible to achieve the EFA targets and goals without reinforcing the non-formal education system, especially in poor countries.

The book provides an introduction to the concepts of literacy and non-formal education and explains in simple terms the planning, management and monitoring of non-formal and adult education programmes by grassroots level representatives of the local government. Several concepts are defined in simple language and their use developed within the activities.

The book has been specifically designed to help educational trainers and policy makers to understand the basic concepts of non-formal education and literacy; roles and responsibilities of local government in non-formal education; general methods and techniques in the planning, management, implementation, monitoring and evaluation of NFE and literacy programmes at the grassroots level.

Contents

1

Introduction

Non-formal education became part of the international discourse on education policy in the late 1960s and early 1970s. It can be seen as related to the concepts of recurrent and lifelong learning. Whereas the latter concepts have to do with the extension of education and learning throughout life, non-formal education is about 'acknowledging the importance of education, learning and training which takes place outside recognized educational institutions'.

In the 1970s, four characteristics came be associated with non-formal education:

— Relevance to the needs of disadvantaged groups.

— Concern with specific categories of person.

— A focus on clearly defined purposes.Flexibility in organization and methods.

In many northern countries the notion of non-formal education is not common in internal policy debates - preferred alternatives being community education and community learning, informal education and social pedagogy.

In 1967 at an international conference in Williamsburg USA, ideas were set out for what was to become a widely read analysis of the growing 'world educational crisis'. There was concern about unsuitable curricula; a realization that educational growth and economic growth were not necessarily in step, and that jobs did not emerge directly as a result of educational inputs.

Many countries were finding it difficult (politically or economically) to pay for the expansion of formal education.The conclusion was that formal educational systems had adapted too slowly to the socio-economic changes around them and that they were held back not only by their own conservatism, but also by the inertia of societies themselves. If we also accept that educational policy making tends to follow rather than lead other social trends, then it followed that change would have to come not merely from within formal schooling, but from the wider society and from other sectors within it. It was from this point of departure that planners and economists in the World Bank began to make a distinction between informal, non-formal and formal education. At around the same time there were moves in UNESCO toward lifelong education and notions of 'the learning society' which culminated in Learning to Be, The Faure Report', UNESCO 1972. Lifelong learning was to be the 'master concept' that should shape educational systems. What emerged was an influential tripartite categorization of learning systems:

— *Formal education*: the hierarchically structured, chronologically graded 'education system', running from primary school through the university and including, in addition to general academic studies, a variety of specialised programmes and institutions for full-time technical and professional training.

— *Informal education*: the truly lifelong process whereby every individual acquires attitudes, values, skills and knowledge from daily experience and the educative influences and resources in his or her environment - from family and neighbours, from work and play, from the market place, the library and the mass media.

— *Non-formal education*: any organised educational activity outside the established formal system - whether operating separately or as an important feature of some broader activity - that is intended to serve identifiable learning clienteles and learning objectives.

Formal education is linked with schools and training institutions; non-formal with community groups and other organizations; and informal covers what is left, e.g. interactions with friends, family and work colleagues. The problem with this is that people often organize educational events as part of their everyday experience and so the lines blur rapidly. These definitions do not imply hard and fast categories. In particular, there may well be some overlap between the informal and the non-formal.

Dividing formal education from out of school education or so-called non-formal education is artificial in many ways. But in some countries, this division reflects the gulf between government provision through the school system, on the one hand, and the needs and interests of marginal populations who are most alienated from the system on the other.

The range of initiatives and programmes that have adopted the title 'non-formal' are many and various. They include literacy and basic education for adults and young people, political and trade union education, 'catching-up' programmes for school drop outs, pre-school education for young children, political and trade union education and various kinds of educational work linked with development initiatives including agricultural extension and training programmes and health education. They also shade over into various examples of both state and private vocational training programmes.

An education system based around schooling could not be sustained because of the sheer cost to already fragile economies. A search for 'new' techniques was therefore on. Within the north it was becoming clear that the school was only one amongst many potential educative elements.

Concepts such as 'the learning society' were gaining some currency. There was the impact of movements such as that of deschooling. At the same time a number of socialist countries initiated large programmes for changing the consciousness, skills and organizations of their populations. They typically used many of the forms that we now label as non-formal education, Specially trained educators sent out to local villages etc to set up and run programmes and recruit further helpers and group members.

The use of mass media such as radio and television, things like newsheets and comics. Provision on a mass scale - a whole region or country is targeted. Sometimes formal, sometimes informal sanctions against those who did not participate. Many of these programmes apparently met with considerable success. In this respect Russia, Cuba, Tanzania, Somalia, Ethiopia and Nicaragua were often quoted as having organised successful mass campaigns - particularly in respect of literacy.

By the mid 1970s a number of non-socialist countries were beginning to turn to the idea of mass non-formal education. It was clear that there remained a large scale and apparently growing problem of illiteracy. It was also clear that economic and social development depended on bringing about changes in many people's thinking.

The development process is in fact an educational process, or rather it should unfailingly be viewed as such. We cannot therefore conceive of development in the absence of education any more than education in the absence of development.

There was a further shift amongst the donor agencies working in the South. Whereas there had been a great emphasis on the provision of plant, and particularly prestigious projects, there was a growing realization that development primarily depended on the people themselves and that much more stress should be placed on improving their quality of life.

This called for new approaches to formal education; it also gave considerable impetus to non-formal education, and especially to basic education for those who had been largely neglected - the urban and rural poor. The problem was that these sorts of programmes had not been tried in the market and political conditions associated with Southern capitalist societies.

Contrasts between 'formal' and 'non-formal' programmes

Simkins T., analysed non-formal education programme in terms of purposes, timing, content delivery systems and control, and contrasted these with formal educational programmes. The resulting ideal-types provide a useful framework - and bring out the extent to which non-formal education initiatives, while emphasizing flexibility, localness and responsiveness remain located within a curricula form of education.

Table. 1: Ideal-type models of normal and non-formal education

	formal	*non-formal*
purposes	Long-term & general Credential-based	Short-term & specific Non-credential-based
timing	long cycle / preparatory / full-time	short cycle / recurrent / part-time
content	standardized/input centred academic entry requirements determine clientele	individualized /output centred practical clientele determine entry requirements
delivery system	institution-based, isolated from environment. rigidly structured, teacher-centred and resource intensive	environment-based, flexible, learner-centred and resource saving
	community related.	
control	external/hierarchical	self-governing/democratic

According to Fordham. P., one of the enduring themes in the literature of non-formal education, has been that the education provided should be in the interests of the learners and that the organization and curriculum planning should preferably be undertaken by the learners themselves: that it should be 'bottom up'. It is also often argued that this should empower learners to understand and if necessary change the social structure around them. According to him Examples where there is a genuine sense of ownership are not easy to find; and almost all have an element of community outreach as part of the general organization. On the other hand examples of top-down non-formal programmes are all too common. Almost all employer-led and State provided training falls into this category.

In this way formal education would broadly approximate to top-down curriculum formation

— non-formal to bottom-up or negotiated curriculum formation

— informal education would arguably be a non-curriculum or conversational form. In respect of literacy programmes, there are a number of dimensions that have proved to be crucial to effectiveness:

— Training and motivation of literacy workers.

— The quality and relevance of materials.

— The reinforcements of literacy.

It is clear from the studies of literacy campaigns that both the commitment and skills of literacy promoters are very important. Enthusiasm is not enough. It is not that straightforward to facilitate learner participation in dialogue and discussion. Certain skills are needed to put across ideas and so on. Many of the literacy workers are young. This meant that they need not be automatically accepted or appreciated.

In some campaigns there has been a considerable effort to try to recruit older workers and those who are known and held in good regard in a locality. In .many campaigns workers are paid, and the job accords them some status. Where volunteers are recruited, for example in the Kenyan initiative, and who live in the local communities, the main incentive is often the hope that this might lead to a full time job.

Most of the various national literacy campaigns have had some central unit which developed materials etc for the workers etc. to use. To this must be added things like the production of regular radio programmes to support initiatives. However, this is both expensive and sophisticated and it is not proved that easy, for example, to update and change materials quite as has been needed.

Once people achieve basic literacy, whatever its precise form, the process creates further demands for post-literacy education, whether to 'catch up' on missed formal education, or to develop organizational or practical skills. At this point things can become quite expensive and complex. The demands are now more sophisticated. To these specific questions must be added some further problems. To begin with, given that initiatives involve voluntary participation - how are people to be attracted on sufficient scale. This is much less of a problem in systems where there is large scale schooling some legal basis for attendance. The successful campaign in Botswana, for example, touched about 20 per cent of the population - it still left quite a few people illiterate. In addition, unless the school system is discredited for some political reason, a lower valuation tends to be put on non-formal education, especially for young people.

Complementarity Between Formal and Non-formal Education

The idea of complementarity between formal and non-formal education is reflected in the national Policy of education. Article 45 of Indian Constitution enjoins upon the provision of free, compulsory and universal education upto the age of 14 years. Both the systems are attempting to fulfil the constitutional obligation of universal elementary education. The New Education Policy has also recommended to coordinate the network of non-formal education fully for realising the target of universal education by 1990 upto the age of 11 years and by 1995 upto the age of 14 years. The responsibility for implementing the above obligation rests with the Ministry of Human Resources development. It, however, also seeks support from other Ministries.

Complementarity lies with the objectives of formal and non-formal education. Both the system of formal and non-formal education aim at improving the quality of life and raising the living standards. The major objectives of the system is to develop the personality of the child through inculcating values, attitudes and other necessary skills of life so that the children can become productive members of the society. Conceptually, there is complementarity between both the system in terms of achieving the objectives of human resources development. Non-formal education has been introduced to cater the needs of out-of-school children who are either drop-out from formal schools at various stages or have never been to school who could not avail of the facilities provided by the formal system due to socio-economic compulsions. It also intends to meet the essential learning needs of children living in remote and sparsely populated areas where the establishment of the formal school is considered to be non-viable.

The character of flexibility brings complementarity in both the systems. Non-formal education has character of flexibility in respect of timings, vacations, curriculum and multiple point entry, etc. and adjustment according to local specific needs of the area and locality. The formal set up is also following the character of flexibility and encouraging multiple point entry. School hours, school vacations and curriculum are adjusted according to needs of the community. However, the practices vary from state to state. The Delhi School Education Act 1973, specifically permits multiple point entry of students. It has been observed that such a provision is generally used for the purpose of allowing transfer of students from one formal school to another at different stages of education. The state of Uttar Pradesh has positive attitude towards formal and non-formal education. The students from non-formal education centres are allowed to appear at class V examination with the students of formal schools and are allowed to join class VI in formal schools after qualifying the examination.

Clientele in the non-formal education are either drop-outs or non-attending children. The students who are drop-outs are from formal schooling. In most of the states teachers are also from the formal schools who teach in non-formal education centres. They are getting additional payment for working in these centres. Regarding the training of the teachers, services of the same teacher educators, lecturers, principals and resources persons are utilized in training the teachers from the State Institute of Education, Universities, Training Colleges and Resources Centres in both the systems. Regarding supervision and inspection, mostly same supervisory staff of the formal set up is deployed for these NFE centres.

District Education Officers (DEO) and District Inspectors of school (DIS) supervise and inspect these NFE centres also from time to time. At the Directorate level, in some states services of the same Director of Public Instruction (DPI) has been utilized for looking after the work of both the formal and non-formal education. Curriculum also plays vital role in establishing the complementarity between formal and non-formal education because the standard in any of the system can't be lower than that of the other.

It is emphasised in New Education Policy that all necessary measures will be taken to ensure that the quality of non-formal education is comparable with formal education. No doubt, the curriculum is based on the demand and need of the people as it is local specific and problem based.

Relevance, practicability and flexibility are the main criterion for the NFE curriculum. Health, vocation, environment, social awareness literacy and numeracy are the dimensions of the NFE curriculum. These criterion is must for NFE but it may be followed in the formal set up also. The aim of both the curricula is to enable the child to acquire certain competencies, skills and knowledge at the primary and middle stages. Besides this the content of education in formal and non-formal sectors has been generally centered around certain learning outcomes expected to be attained by the learners at the end of primary/elementary stage.

The attainment of learners are evaluated on the basis of the learning outcomes specified in the Minimum Learning Continuum (MLC) developed by the NCERT. It has also attempted that the content should be derived from the real situations in both formal and non-formal education. In addition to this, a common machinery is being prepared the instructional materials and curriculum for formal and non-formal education.

The NCERT is preparing the curriculum and instructional material at the national level and SIE, SISE, SCERT, SIERT and SRC are preparing the curriculum at the state level. In most of the state M.P. Model condensed version of formal curriculum is being utilised in the non-formal education. The methodology used in the NFE is different from formal education and different pedagogical strategies have been utilised to cater the needs of the children in both the systems. The teachers in NFE centres are generally deployed from the formal set up and they teach in both the system according to the needs and situation of the students.

In both the system the teacher rearrange the content according to the needs of students and is also free to use available resources in teaching. Teacher helps the children in preparing teaching aids like charts, album, drawing cards, free hand sketching, wood toys and clay toys etc. in both the systems according to their situations. Media is common strategy in both the system. Dialogue, role playing, simulation, group discussion and problem solving are the teaching methods commonly used in both formal and non-formal education.

The theoretical and practical knowledge of vocational skills is also provided effectively in non-formal centres through socially useful productive work (SUPW) because the children in the centres are coming from such homes, where they are already busy with such activities like agriculture, fisheries bamboo and woodwork etc. Except this, like formal school curriculum and co-curricular activities are also organised in NFE centres.

Another important means to integrate formal and non-formal education is mass-media. The educational programmes of both the systems are fruitfully broadcasted by INSAT 1-B which is already in operation in the country. Twenty either stations of the All India Radio (AIR) have already been linked with the INSAT based radio net work. Special equipment has been installed at these stations to receive programmes directly from the satellite. The programmes of education both in schools and NFE centres will be imparted through Radio as well as TV network meaningfully.UNICEF aided project on mass-media is being implemented by the NCERT in collaborations with the state governments.

In the education sector UNICEF-assisted projects are being implemented to provide relevant curriculum and methodology for both the systems to promote the universalisation of elementary education by NCERT in collaboration with state education departments. The projects include:Early Childhood Education (ECE), primary Education Curriculum Renewal (PECR), Comprehensive Access to primary Education (CAPE), Nutrition, Health, Education and Environmental Senitation (NHEES), Development Activities in Community Education and Participation (DACEP), etc. Through these projects new contents and methods using environment oriented and problem solving approaches are being developed for both formal and non-formal education.

Basic skill training consists of literacy, numeracy and technology in other words communication, life and productive skill is being imparted to both the system of formal and non-formal education. According to the recommendations of national Council for Teacher Education (NCTE), most of the states have modified the primary teacher education curriculum to prepare would-be-teachers for both the system through the same process. Under the UNICEF-assisted project Comprehensive Access to Primary Education (CAPE) of NCERT, the learning material for the out of schools children is being prepared following the approach training-cum-production and this approach has been introduced in the curriculum of teacher training institutes in different states. The teacher trainee has to prepare relevance-based learning materials, i.e. capsule and module.

In some of the states non-formal education centres are attached to the primary teacher training institute for orienting the trainees about the functioning of non-formal education. In addition to this, non-formal education has been envisioned in pre-service training. Teachers from formal set up are being provided training about the functioning of non-formal education through in-service training and short-term course organised by the State Institute of Education, (SIE), State Institute of Science Education (SISE), State Council of Educational Research and Training (SCERT), State Institute of Educational Research and Training (SIERT) and State Resources Centres (SRC) etc.. The erstwhile Centre of Education Technology (CET) now called Central Institute of Educational Technology (CIET), a constituent of NCERT, under the project 'Satellite Instructional Television Experiment (SITE) provided training to 4,8000 primary school teachers in one year in both content of science and approach of science teaching.

The Bureau of School Education of Ministry of Human Resources Development (MHRD) is administering both the type of education at the national level. NCERT as an academic wing of MHRD coordinate academic activities of both the systems and prepare curriculum and methodology according to needs and problems. The administrative set up for formal and non-formal education, however, differs from state to state. Three types of administrative models are functioning at the state level. In some states formal and non-formal education are administered by the Directorate of Adult Education and still in some others formal, non-formal and adult education come within preview of one single Directorate of Education. At the district level in the States, District Education Officers and District inspector of Schools are practically looking after the work of supervision and inspection of non-formal education. In these states, where non-formal education has been tagged with adult education, the administration, supervision and inspection are looked after by the District Adult Education Officers. Block Education Officers and Extension Education Officers are responsible for looking after the job of supervision and inspection of both the system at block level.

Village Education Committee and parent Teacher Association are responsible for the management, supervision and inspection of both the system at village level. School complex is also an important means to strengthen integrated functioning of schools and non-formal education centres. In each complex there is a central school which is generally a high/higher secondary school in which about ten to twelve primary schools and about five to seven middle schools within the radius of five to seven kilometers participated within a month or fortnightly.

All sorts of difficulties regarding administration, management, curriculum, methodology and other problems of implementation of various programmes in both formal and non-formal education are discussed in the complex meetings and all possible help is provided by the central school to solve their problems.

Both the set-ups shares facilities and resources in NCERT, Universities, Teacher Training Institutions, SIE, SCERT and SRC etc. are used by both the systems for academic guidance and consultations services, seminars, short-term courses, conferences, and training courses are organised in the above institutions for both formal and non-formal education.

Most of the NFE centres are also running in the school buildings in the evenings though at some places these are running in temples, churches, mosques, community centres and dharamshala etc. Besides this surveys are conducted in respect of boys and girls for organising the NFE centres and reports are maintained. Attendance registers are maintained for checking the regularity of the students. Stock registers, teacher diaries are also kept for judging the progress of the children.Non-formal education is also financed by the Ministry of Human Resources Development like formal education. The MHRD provides grants to nine educationally backward states on the basis of 50:50, 90:10 in case of exclusively for girls and hundred per cent in case of voluntary organisation for running these NFE centres. Teacher's salaries, student remuneration, and contingent grants are paid out of these grants. Though the teachers are paid much less as compared to the formal school teachers but this is effective way of utilising the limited resources of the nation for meeting the ever increasing demands of the people.

Evaluation of both the systems enforces complementarity. Children though in NFE system are not only evaluated in terms of performance in examination like formal system but in terms of personality development like social, emotional and mental, etc. The children are compared and evaluated with themselves viz, with their previous achievement at different levels.

2

Non-formal Education Development

The vast majority of developing countries in the south have remained locked into positions in the international economic order which impose constraints on national decision-making of a quite different magnitude from those which affect most countries in the North. In the 1980s these inequalities in power and influence were brought into sharper focus by a global recession and a widespread debt crisis among developing countries.

A study covering 107 developing countries, of which forty-one were categorized as 'least developed countries', found that between 1980 and 1990 there were significant falls for most 'developing countries' in gross domestic product, public expenditure and private consumption per head. The latter decreased in 81 per cent of the least developed countries and in 64 per cent of other developing countries.

The United Nations reports that more than 2.8 billion people, close to half the world's population, live on less than the equivalent of $2/day. More than 1.2 billion people, or about 20 per cent of the world population, live on less than the equivalent of $1/day. South Asia has the largest number of poor people (522 million of whom live on less than the equivalent of $1/ day). Sub-Saharan Africa has the highest proportion of people who are poor, with poverty affecting 46.3 per cent or close to half of the regions' population.

Between 1950 and 1970, the numbers of those enrolled in schools rose dramatically on a global level, and literacy levels rose, though not as rapidly as had been hoped. Rural communities, and especially rural women, still missed out on educational opportunities. None the less, the hope was that access to education would deliver many benefits: for the nation, a skilled work force to contribute to economic development, national unity and social cohesion, and in some countries, popular participation in politics. For the individual, it promised an escape from poverty, greater social prestige and mobility, and the prospect of a good job, preferably in town. In practice these hopes were often unfulfilled, particularly among the least privileged social groups, but they remained powerful aspirations.

In many countries of the South the debt crisis of the 1980s ended an era of unprecedented growth for education. Countries severely affected by the economic crisis, often compounded by military and political conflict, saw the numbers of children enrolling in school fall, and a marked increase in dropout rates among children who do start school. They saw a decline in opportunities for young people and adults to participate in education. More recently, the situation has generally improved in a number of countries - although, most significantly, not in sub-Saharan Africa.

The United Nations reports that worldwide:

— The number of children in school has risen significantly, from 599 million in 1990 to 681 million in 1998.

— Since 1990, some 10 million more children go to school every year, which is nearly double the 1980-90 average.

— East Asia, the Pacific, Latin America and the Caribbean are close to achieving universal primary education.

— The number of out-of-school children decreased from 127 million in 1990 to 113 million in 1998. In Latin America and the Caribbean, for example, the number of out-of-school children was halved, from 11.4 million in 1990 to 4.8 million in 1998.

— The number of children in pre-school education has risen by 5 per cent in the past decade. Some 104 million children were enrolled in pre-primary establishments in 1998.

— The number of literate adults doubled from 1970 to 1998 from 1.5 billion to 3.3 billion. Today, 85 per cent of all men and 74 per cent of all women can read and write.

— Some 87 per cent of young adults (15-24 years olds) are literate worldwide

— Despite progress in actual numbers, illiteracy rates remain too high: at least 875 million adults remain illiterate, of which 63.8 per cent are women – exactly the same proportion as 10 years ago.

Given the scale of indebtedness and the lack of internal funds for education and social programmes, Southern countries have become particularly dependent on assessments and perspectives made by key international and national agencies in the north. Here the various reviews and policy analyses undertaken or sponsored by the World Bank have been particularly influential.

Discussion of the dominance of external visions of education inevitably brings us to questions of colonialism and imperialism. Colonialism in its most traditional sense involves the gaining of control over particular geographical areas and is usually associated with the with the exploitation of various areas in the world by European powers from about 1500 on. It is often used interchangeably with 'imperialism'. Colonialism commonly involves the settlement of the controlling population in a territory; and the exploitation of local economic resources for metropolitan use. It has taken many forms ranging from models of assimilation e.g. France and Portugal where the occupying power has sought make the colony more formally part of their system and culture; to more segregational approaches such as that adopted by Britain.

Neo-colonialism is usually taken as referring to the economic situation of former colonies post-independence. Here the basic argument runs something like the following. Political de-colonization did little or nothing to alter the economic balance between states and the power of western (and now eastern) capital. International law, institutions such as the World Bank (and banks in general), corporate property rights and the operation of world markets has left control in the hands of the elites in the former metropolitan powers. Under neo-colonialism, as under direct colonial rule, the relationship between the centre and the periphery... is said to involve the export of capital from the former to the latter; a reliance on Western manufactured goods and services which thwarts indigenous development efforts; further deterioration in the terms of trade for the newly independent countries; and a continuation of the process of cultural Westernization which guarantee the West's market outlets elsewhere in the world. the operations of transnational corporations in the Third World are seen as the principal agents of contemporary neo-colonialism since these are seen as exploiting local resources and influencing international trade and national governments to their own advantage.

The linkage of economic change and education; and the interest of the World Bank in such developments would appear to support the thesis that education initiatives can be the agent of colonialism. This is certainly the case for schools. Schools are *colonialistic* in that they attempt to impose economic and political relationships in the society *especially* on those children who gain least (or lose most) from those relationships. Schools demand the most passive response from those groups in society who are the most oppressed by the economic and political system, and allow the most active participation and learning from those who are least likely to want change. While this is logical in preserving the status quo, it is also a means of colonializing children to accept unsatisfactory roles. In its colonialistic characterization, schooling helps develop colonizer-colonized relationships between individuals and between groups in society. It formalizes these relationships, giving them a logic that makes reasonable the unreasonable.

The colonial element in schooling (or in informal and non-formal education initiatives) being the attempt to silence particular ways of speaking about the world. To this extent one class or group could be said to colonize another. Sometimes the term domestic or internal colonialism is used to describe such exploitative relationships between the 'centre' (the metropolis) and the 'periphery' (the satellite) of particular societies or nation states. There have been problems around such usage - especially as colonialism has tended to be used in relation to the exploitation of majority populations by minority groups. However, as a metaphor it remains a highly suggestive one - especially as it dramatizes the links with imperial powers. As well as direct economic and political arrangements, colonialism also involves powerful cultural forces, in particular, language.

In an attempt to escape the association of blackness with evil, the black man dons a white mask, or thinks of himself as a universal subject equally participating in a society that advocates an equality supposedly abstracted from personal appearance. Cultural values are internalized, or "epidermalized" into consciousness, creating a fundamental disjuncture between the black man's consciousness and his body. Under these conditions, the black man is necessarily alienated from himself.

Many of the adult (and non-formal) education programmes associated with 'post-independence' governments looked to combat 'colonial mentalities' and to further a commitment to the emerging nation state. Another overt example of an anti-colonialist programme was Cuba's *Schools in the Countryside* initiative which had as one of its objectives, 'to eliminate economic, political and cultural dependence on the United States'. Certainly, non-formal education initiatives became associated with work that was self-consciously 'relevant' to the needs of disadvantaged groups. A number of those involved as educators were concerned with reducing poverty, increasing equity and about greater equality in the distribution of power and resources, but were constrained by political circumstance.

Many popular education programmes have had a clear emphasis on social mobilization and political development. Churches, unions and groups within social movements have been involved in such initiatives - and there has, in some at least, been a concern to resist unwarranted state intervention into civic life. However, not all informal and non-formal educational initiatives have been so focused on social and political justice. Indeed, it could be said that many have been rather more concerned with creating conditions for capitalist advancement. Often this nas been wrapped up with a desire to stimulate economic growth and development, but it can end up either advantaging investors (frequently from the former colonial powers) or having little impact on growth.

Literacy has become associated in the minds of some policy makers with development. During the 1980s and 1990s, political conflicts as much as economic problems have sharpened awareness of the issues in non-formal education. Literacy is seen as a political issue by many governments. High illiteracy figures are often regarded as revealing failures in their education systems. Governments of all political persuasions have, therefore, made at least sporadic efforts to promote literacy among adults, sometimes with substantial funding from international organizations. They frequently made significant use of non-formal programmes. In the 1970s there was a fairly widespread belief that literacy was a sound economic investment which would lead to increased productivity.

In the recessionary climate of the 1980s, the short-term returns on literacy were called into question, and generally speaking the long-term rewards of education received less attention. Furthermore, with high levels of unemployment, there are usually sufficient literate candidates for the shrinking numbers of jobs requiring literacy. The outcomes of government-sponsored literacy programmes and campaigns have been extremely mixed. Literacy work has largely taken two forms. Short campaigns involving mass mobilization have been one method.

Literacy programmes involving ongoing work over a period years, either nationally or targeting selected communities or regions, have been the other. In societies undergoing major political change, 'revolutionary governments' have been generally more able to mobilize people both to teach and to learn. In countries where there is little popular identification with the regime, especially under authoritarian governments, efforts at literacy promotion may be regarded with suspicion or even contempt.

It is in these circumstances that non-governmental literacy initiatives have become a focus of interest. It could be argued that greater community involvement and organization may generate challenges to the government - demands for democracy, land reform, and greater access to services such as education. However, one of the key outcomes of such literacy programmes is that they, and the aid that sustains them, work to legitimate capitalist development and social inequality.

In the light of academic reseraches and surveys we can see that three key further trends around literacy are emetging in the developing countries.

— *A move from a concern with literacy alone to a concern with the schooling-literacy interrelationship.* In some of the literature there has been an assumption that as people become more literate they will encourage their children to go to school. There has been little or no research done of this - and indeed the reverse process may be more relevant. What has been of particular concern to the World Bank and others was that the ability of primary schooling to attract and hold its clienteles was faltering. For as long as primary school enrolments were rising as a percentage of the population then it was possible to believe that over the course of a generation illiteracy would been eliminated. In Africa there is now evidence of declining participation in schooling. A further factor in some places has been the levying of fees as the income from taxes and aid has decreased. There have also been worries around the quality of primary schooling in a number of states - particularly those that are poor. Lacking textbooks, adequate facilities and teachers the idea of a full primary education is rather remote.

— *The reassertion of achievable measures of school and adult literacy.* In looking at the achievements of both primary schooling and literacy work a basic question is posed: what is the level of basic education for all, including adults, that should be set as a minimum in order to retain elementary literacy skills? There has been an increased interest in the setting of standard measures of performance and here the World Bank has been active. This shift along with the others is sometimes referred to as the 'new realism'.

— *A move from the campaign literature to the analysis of literacy realities.* There are still very few detailed and textured studies of work in particular countries or regions. There does seem to have been a shift in the literature however, to more grounded discussions of literacy - and less of the rhetorical, exhortorary material.

Non-formal Education Initiatives

Today, we can gain information and knowledge through the media, our workplaces, and community activities. Nonformal education offers hands-on experiences as well as more traditional modes of learning. Systematic approaches are needed to help educational consumers sort through and tie together the information resulting from everyday experiences. A list of initiatives which should be taken to enhance the non-formal education programmes are listed belw.

1. *Expand public access to opportunities to learn about sustainability issues as they relate to the private, work, and community lives of individuals. Support a campaign to raise public awareness of sustainability, convey information on indicators of sustainable development, and encourage individuals to adopt sustainable practices in their daily lives.*

   Today, information about the global environment, and sustainable development is increasingly available through television, print media, telecommunications networks, and commercial software products. Using this information we can make decisions about day-today actions on what to buy and what to do about issues that affect their communities. Although the public has a heightened awareness of sustainability issues and is responding by making wise decisions regarding those issues, the process of sifting through information is not as easy or helpful as many would like. Unclear messages increase the difficulty of encouraging an individual (or targeted audience) to engage in action or make informed choices. School systems are struggling to develop and implement the requisite curricula to teach youngsters about the importance of sustainability and its relationship to quality of life. Businesses, community groups, and professional organizations have engaged in this dialogue and have been quick to realize that more information is needed.

A concerted public awareness effort will assist public in gaining a firm grasp of the concept of sustainability and the practices that promote it. The program should employ specific examples of everyday actions that are sustainable, descriptive, potential cumulative benefits associated with sustainable behavior, and the positive impacts of changed policies and practices on the world as a whole. If these efforts are successful, individuals will understand that these changes are worthwhile and have the potential to raise the quality of their lives. Easily understood information should be shared on a regular basis. This information should include relevant measures to gauge societal progress towards sustainability.

2. *Support a system of regularly updated, comprehensible national benchmarks of progress toward the goals of sustainability.*

Throughout the world, decisions are made that affect the long-term health and viability of communities. These decisions are responses to growth and development issues and the use and protection of natural resources. Individual citizens often sense a gap between their own day-to-day choices and the impact on events at the broader community, national, or global scales. With help from the media, a focused partnership aimed at informing the public about indicators of sustainability can help bridge this gap. The indicators can provide citizens with information that demonstrates individual contributions to the overall picture. Such efforts are under discussion, but no one best formula has been found to date. With further discussion, however, a system of benchmarks will emerge that can play a significant role in informing individuals.

3. *Entertainment media may consider designing a coordinated media campaign to raise youngsters' awareness of sustainability.*

   Entertainment media can play a role in raising the awareness of young children about a concept like sustainability. Young people around the world are playing a role in monitoring progress toward sustainable development through the Sustainability Indicators Project, which is sponsored by the United Nations. Under this project, youth help measure progress toward building and maintaining healthy communities. The Sustainability Indicators Project is spearheaded by *Rescue Mission: Planet Earth,* an organization with affiliates throughout the world. School groups, individuals, community groups, and families are invited to participate in the project. The kinds of questions the program is trying to address include: "What is happening in your community?" "Are people becoming more prosperous while at the same time healing and conserving the environment?" Sustainable Development Indicators are based on the broad issues discussed in *Agenda 21* and involve looking at specific environmental or social issues, pinpointing trends through analysis.

4. *Support the continued outreach to American journalists on issues related to sustainability.*

   Efforts have been launched to inform the journalism community in a systematic way about issues of global environmental concern. Examples include *The Reporter's Environmental Handbook* , published by the New Jersey Institute of Technology and *Reporting Climate Change* , published by the National Safety Council. Such efforts have been limited, however, and require additional resources and a broader base of information on current, accurate findings.

5. *Establish incentive programs, such as national awards, to recognize successful partnerships within the business community that support educational efforts on sustainability.*

   The private sector, especially the business community, has been responsible for some of the most innovative programs in the environmental and sustainable development arena. Nevertheless, school personnel struggle to establish successful partnerships to tap the expertise of the business and industry community. At the same time, businesses are searching to identify the best educational approaches. Incentives are needed to encourage and sustain partnerships and successes that are working. Recognition for those who are investing resources and creative energy in the formation and implementation of educational programs can encourage others if they believe that their work will be publicly acknowledged.

If the public is to become more involved in local sustainability issues, support mechanisms are needed to translate research information, transfer new technologies, introduce educational strategies, develop public policy, and organize at the community level to chart sustainable courses of action. A successful extension network would empower individuals in communities to shape their own futures through an appropriate mix of education, technical assistance, and fiscal support. Extension networks give individuals the tools to control their own futures, while providing data and information, educational expertise, and needed financial assistance.

6. *Establish national sustainable development extension networks to foster access to information, technical expertise, and collaborative strategies that result in action taken by local communities.*

These sustainable development extension network could employ services offered by diverse educational units such as community colleges, public schools, and private sector educational entities, as well as nongovernmental organizations focusing on similar issues and priorities. The existing extension system could contribute to the new sustainable development extension networks by providing technical assistance that brings together researchers who are developing new technologies and those who adopt those new technologies; promoting sustainable development practices by providing information on sustainable alternatives and benefits; facilitating community visioning and planning processes; and providing access to current data and information available through electronic gateways.

A sustainable development extension network could:

- Assist in the implementation of a national effort to increase awareness of sustainability at the state and community levels.
- Identify, document, and electronically link community civic groups, schools, businesses, and other entities interested in sustainable development.
- Provide for local and state participation in the development of essential learnings in sustainability, design of community visioning and assessment processes, student performance outcomes, criteria for curriculum development, and other standards.
- Coordinate the efforts of major groups that design community visioning and assessment processes by documenting strategies and compiling results of such efforts.
- Identify model programs that satisfy agreed-upon standards of sustainable development.
- Design and deliver training to organizations and individuals interested in applying principles of sustainability to their businesses, governments, projects, families, or schools.

— Develop a five-year plan of action that targets specific geographic areas through a priority-setting process, and recommend public policy that enables the actions.

— Develop a multidimensional matrix that includes environmental, economic, and social components so each agency role will be maximized in terms of education, technical support, and financial assistance to specific geographic areas.

— Coordinate the above functions with new and existing clearinghouses related to education for sustainability across the world.

Although the goal might be reached more quickly through unilateral investment in a single organizational entity, the national goal of sustainable development requires a more comprehensive strategy. Representatives from the participating agencies as well as state consortia should direct a process to determine how a sustainable development extension network can best be managed, staffed, and financed.

The formation, structure, management, leadership, and implementation of a sustainable development extension network could be based on the following principles:

— Research-based technology is generated and applied as determined by community needs.

— Transfer of technology to communities and individuals is based on an appropriate combination of education plus technical and financial support aimed at user adoption.

— Management processes for identifying needs, setting priorities, and building coalitions and partnerships are inclusionary.

— Targeted and focused assistance responds directly to local communities and needs.

— Existing research, education, and extension management and delivery systems are utilized, redefined, and expanded.

— Alternative implementation strategies and organizational participation models are provided.

— Consistency in substance among programs and the results from programs are based on a verified set of principles and outcomes.

— Management and design of the structure and process are not dominated by any one entity, but developed through a collaborative process of defining common goals and unique organizational roles.

In 1991, a group of US federal agencies initiated a unique voluntary approach to pollution prevention in rural areas. The Farm Assessment System and Home Assessment System has a simple goal: with technical assistance from the agencies, landowners increase their knowledge of health- and non-health-related risks from pollution, look critically at their property, and then take voluntary actions to reduce the risks. To date, more than 22,000 individual assessments have been conducted by farmers, rural homeowners, and ranchers. Actions they have taken to reduce risks on their property range from improving indoor air quality to reducing lead levels in drinking water and improving petroleum storage and pesticides handling. Participants have invested more than $15 million to reduce environmental risks. The success of the program lies in its flexible framework and the local support it generates.

7. *Encourage partnerships and activities that support community visioning and assessment activities.*

   Visioning processes enable communities to plan for the long-term health of their communities and make decisions that will determine the economic viability of their communities. Many communities across the world have taken this challenge seriously and are engaged in a process of visioning and assessment leading to strategic planning. Local decision-making can be enhanced with information and technical assistance from state and federal governments. At the international level, Chapter 28 of *Agenda 21* of the 1992 United Nations Conference on Environment and Development (UNCED) charged communities with formulating action plans to move toward a sustainable future. This process calls for the broadest possible public participation, with representatives from diverse areas coming together to define sustainability on the local level and support plans and projects that will implement their communities' visions.

8. *Create a national program in partnership with organizations that will provide educational resources and leadership training in support of community visioning and assessment.*

   National support of visioning processes can include facilitating the exchange of ideas by providing appropriate and timely information about successful models for replication; training of leaders for visioning processes; expansion of local, regional, national, and international visioning networks; and engagement of communities across the world in integrated, holistic approaches to long-term planning for sustainable communities. A national program such as this could include the following four components:

— Identifying and compiling examples of visioning processes that have been successful in communities;

— Designing and developing a workbook and other resource materials for dissemination to interested communities to serve as a guidebook for action and planning at the community level;

— Establishing a Leadership Institute for Sustainable Communities to train leaders in facilitating cooperative planning by diverse stakeholders; and

— Establishing a council through the proposed Sustainable Development Extension Network to coordinate efforts at the state and federal levels in support of community visioning activities.

A number of communities are in various stages of defining their future and are employing a variety of visioning approaches. A national clearinghouse could facilitate the sharing of successful strategies from communities of various sizes that are wrestling with challenges in diverse environmental and economic contexts. These successes can serve as models for communities with similar characteristics. The tasks to accomplish this include:

1. Identifying and compiling examples of visioning processes that have been successful in communities.

   — Identifying successful practices, analyzing the processes used, and distilling commonalities into transferable models.

   — Developing print and media materials that illustrate these models and describe methods for replicating visioning and long-term planning processes.

2. Designing and developing a workbook and other resource materials for dissemination to interested communities to serve as a guidebook for action and planning at the community level.

   A structured workbook and other information can aid stakeholders in planning, dialogue, and information gathering at the local level. Indicators of progress or benchmarks described in the workbook could include:

   — Demonstration of investment by partners representing diverse constituencies;

   — Ongoing engagement in a community visioning process or commitment to begin such a process;

   — Definition of the "community," i.e. population center, a coalition of communities in a region, watershed, or ecoregion;

   — Identification of currently existing resources, i.e., constituencies, community resources, and natural resources;

— Design of a mechanism for continuously redefining, reinvesting, and reinventing the community as a self-sustaining entity; and

— Emphasis on continuing education, training, and retooling designed to generate a workforce that is appropriately prepared for new technologies and job opportunities.

3. Establishing a Leadership Institute for Sustainable Communities to train leaders in facilitating cooperative planning by diverse stakeholders.

   Key to the success of community visioning and planning are skillful leadership and advocacy by a few central figures.

   — A "trainer of leaders model" could be developed and implemented as part of the initial phase of encouraging communities to participate in a visioning process with long-term planning toward a sustainable future.

   — The model could emphasize teamwork building, processes for inclusion of all constituencies, group facilitation skills, networking, and volunteerism.

   — Leaders and communities with successful experiences could serve as a cadre of mentors and development teams to transfer knowledge and skills to other leaders in communities with similar needs and characteristics (e.g., sister cities).

4. Establishing a council through the Sustainable Development Extension Network to coordinate

efforts at the state and federal levels in support of community visioning activities.

— The proposed Sustainable Development Extension Network should form a coordinating council with representatives from federal agencies, local and state governments, business and industry, nongovernmental organizations, and professional associations.

— The council should provide a management function at the national level and encourage a coordination function at the state level.

— A streamlined, accessible, and efficient system for enabling communities to request assistance for planning grants, consulting services, community assessments, and educational support should be implemented.

10. *Workforce Development*

The current workforce must have the opportunity to develop the skills needed to work sustainably, and future workers need to be adequately prepared in this area prior to entering the workforce. Training for sustainability will require initiatives at the state and community levels.

The transition from an agricultural to an industrial society and, more recently, to an information society have prompted changes in employment that have not been sufficiently reflected in workforce development programs. Occupations that once offered solid careers are in decline; therefore people who are planning their careers need to assess what skills will be in demand. Employment is expected to reach 147.5 million by 2005, a 12 percent rate of increase over the coming decade. Since job projections are clouded by uncertainties caused by unforeseen changes in technology or the balance of trade, a workforce must be developed that is readily adaptable to change. This need for flexibility and a highly skilled workforce presents a genuine opportunity for educators. If employers are willing to pay more for highly skilled workers, then the quality of education and training should be raised. If linked effectively to careers, the proportion of good jobs can be increased. The challenge is to sustain economic vitality and the quality of life that is sometimes taken for granted.

11. *Disseminate effective school-to-work models that emphasize issues of sustainability while encouraging dialogue with the business sector to address sustainability through hiring and recruitment practices.*

    Because the national school-to-work initiative is built upon business partnerships, it is important for these programs to integrate components of industry-based skill standards. In addition, although many programs are in operation, those that promote sustainability have not been identified. As efforts like these are launched, the business community could provide job opportunities and internships for students who are studying the principles of sustainable development. Attention given to hiring and recruitment practices would help complete the cycle and secure an appropriately trained workforce.

11. *Encourage lifelong learning about sustainability at the individual, household, and community levels.*

Lifelong learning is "adult education for individuals who no longer attend school on a regular, full-time basis." The term *lifelong learning* encompasses adult education for vocational and professional advancement, enjoyment and leisure, and remediation for improving basic skills and knowledge needed to function as a member of a family or community. Although the concept initially focused on community colleges, the idea is spreading to public schools, institutions of higher education, community agencies, proprietary schools, and computer software developers.

The continually changing world in which we live requires that learners of all ages educate themselves throughout their lives. More people than ever before are looking to various forms of lifelong learning opportunities to upgrade their skills and increase their job stability. Continuous learning helps bolster public awareness of the changing global marketplace while encouraging individuals to be more productive and successful citizens. Technology helps adult learners gain greater control over when, where, and how they obtain new skills and knowledge. Computers and telecommunication devices provide new access to learning for remote populations, special populations such as the disabled, and workers on-site and at home. Learning about the concept of sustainability is an ongoing process. Learning opportunities should include the essential learnings of sustainable development and the practical approaches that contribute to sustainable living.

Encouraging lifelong learning about sustainability at the household level depends partly on the extent to which adults are aware and pass on that knowledge.

If parents are lifelong learners, children also are likely to become lifelong learners. When adults take full advantage of the many resources available in their community, they will strengthen the relationship between home and school while enhancing their own work and personal lives. At the community level, libraries are an important force in fostering literacy skills and providing adult part-time education. Community colleges offer a valuable resource as well. Community college programs that serve the needs of the community and strengthen the education of local citizens should be identified and promoted.

12. *Develop community college courses and programs aimed at producing the skills and information needed for contributing to sustainable activities at work and during leisure activities.*

Courses should highlight retraining on practical skills and the changing role of technology. Continued efforts by nonprofit groups, civic organizations, and the business community are needed to ensure that needs responding to a vision of healthy, prosperous neighborhoods and communities are being identified and met.

3

Literacy and Non-formal Education: Status in Developing Countries

Despite the global progress made in terms of quantitative increase in primary education enrolments and literacy rates, major challenge remain. There are still 875 million adult illiterates and 113 million children out-of-school who will eventually join the ranks of adult illiterates unless appropriate educational opportunities are opened to them. In addition, gender disparity continues to permeate education systems, and the quality of learning and the acquisition of human values and skills fall far short of the aspirtions and needs of individuals and societies. These findings led to the international community's collective commitment to pursue a broad-based strategy to ensure that by 2015, all children have access to and complete, free and compulsory primary education of good quality, and to achieve a 50 per cent improvement in levels of adult literacy.

In order to achieve these goals, participants at the World Education Forum called upon all countries to diversify their educational delivery systems in order to meet the learning needs of all. School access and retention in most developing countries have been affected during recent years by number of barriers, involving both in-school and out-of-school factors. In-school factors may include unavailability or inaccessibility of schools owing to distance, poor quality and inefficiency, school process, etc. Out-of-school factors refer mostly to direct costs and opportunity costs.

Many countries have applied different measures to increase school enrolment and retention rates, mainly by attempting to improve the school supply conditions (introducing double/multiple shifts and multigrade classes, increasing class size, encouraging single-sex schooling, incentives to teachers, etc.).

However, most of the demand factors are those operating outside the school policy domain and are unlikely to be affected, in the short and medium terms, by the government educational policies. Some countries have recently experienced a significant increase in enrolment ratios as a result of government commitment to reduce the direct cost by eliminating school fees and/or uniforms, providing learning materials and free textbooks, free or subsidized transportation, and school feeding programmes.

In most cases, the resulting high enrolment ratios were followed by high drop-out rates, mainly attributed to demand factors such as school opportunity costs and limited economic opportunities that affect future earning potential and thus the returns from schooling. Thus, these traditional measures have proven not sufficient to overcome all school barriers, particularly for poor and marginalized groups such as rural groups, girls and ethnic minorities who have abandoned or have difficulties in accommodating to school requirements.

In most countries, non-formal education was found highly effective not only in addressing the inadequacies of formal school in terms of retention and completion rates, adaptability and functionality but also in catering to the learning needs of different target groups, i. e., those children who cannot or do not get enrolled in primary school, those who drop out from school, youths and adults who relapse into illiteracy and those who have never benefited from any schooling.

Due to its flexibility in terms of organisation, schedule and duration, non-formal education has been found relevant in addressing a number of school barriers, especially those related to the educational demand factors. However, non-formal education should not be seen as an alternative education system nor a shortcut to the rapid education of a population. But it has to be recognized as providing a second chance or catch-up learning opportunities to those who missed formal schooling or failed to be attracted by the formal system.

As far as education remains in the heart of the poverty alleviation strategies, non-formal education appears to be particularly helpful in that it enables the rural or urban poor and other marginalized groups to acquire useful knowledge, attitudes and skills. Besides, non-formal education affords wide array of learning opportunities directly associated with income driven activities. Therefore, non-formal education programmes play an important complementary and supplementary role to attaining the EFA goals. Today, most of experts as well as EFA partners agencies are convinced that it is impossible to achieve the EFA targets and goals without reinforcing the non-formal education system, especially in poor countries.

In re-affirming the vision of the World Declaration on Education for All, the participants in the World Education Forum acknowledge the seriousness of the challenge represented by the world's nine high-population countries (E-9) comprising Bangladesh, Brazil, China, Egypt, India, Indonesia, Mexico, Nigeria and Pakistan.

In fact, with 3.2 billion people, these countries account for more than 50 per cent of the world's population and 57 per cent of the world's school-age population. Besides, nearly 50 per cent of the world's out-of-school children and almost 70% of the world's illiterate adults are in these countries. Among these countries, India and China, with respectively 289 million and 152 million illiterate adults, account for more than half of the world's illiterate population.

Despite significant breakthroughs observed during the past decade in all of the nine countries, there still remains a large number of children, youth and adults without access to any form of education necessary for their personal and societal development.

The above realities justify the attention given to the E-9 countries in the global strategy to meet the EFA goals and targets, as any significant progress recorded in these countries immediately affects the world education picture. Of the many initiatives taken so far in order to expand educational opportunities within these countries, the development of non-formal education programmes can be seen as the most effective.

This chapter aims to analyse the status of and trends in the development of adult and non-formal education in the E-9 countries, within the current context of diversifying educational delivery systems in order to achieve the Dakar targets.

Education for All: Trends in E-9 countries

The size and the growth of the population constitute one of the major obstacles for EFA in tE-9 countries, which account altogether for more than half of the world's' population. Population issues are therefore seen as an important elements of the strategies to achieve universal primary education (UPE) in these countries. The total population of the E-9 countries rose from 2.8 billion in 1990 to 3.2 billion in 2000; it is projected to reach 3.6 billion in 2010 and close to 4 billion in 2020. As a main determinant of the socioeconomic demand sector, this population growth has certainly increased resource constraints, in particular as regard the educational infrastructure and funding.

The E-9 countries continue to maintain their share of the world's population. In 1980, they accounted for 52.2 per cent of the world's population and this slightly increased to 53.6 per cent in 2000. This proportion is projected to stagnate up to the year 2020.

Currently, about 55 per cent of the world's population increase takes place in the E-9 countries; this proportion, which was 58 per cent in the period 1980-90 and 57 per cent in 1990-2000, is expected to decrease over time. Despite an increase in the E-9 total population, the average annual growth shows deceleration, in both absolute and relative (growth rate) terms. This trend can be observed in seven of the nine countries, Nigeria and Pakistan being the exceptions.

Although there should be a deceleration in the growth rate of the total population in the next decade, in absolute terms the average annual increment should increase in these two countries. Currently, they are the only two of the E-9 countries that have the annual population growth rate of 2 per cent and over, i. e., 2.3 per cent for Nigeria and 2.5 per cent for Pakistan in the period 2000-2005.

In 2000, China accounted for about 40 per cent of the total E-9 population and India for about 31 per cent. The remaining shares were as follows:

Indonesia	6.5 per cent;
Brazil	5.2 per cent;
Pakistan	4.8 per cent;
Bangladesh	4 per cent;
Nigeria	3.4 per cent;
Mexico	3 per cent;
Egypt	2.1 per cent.

As for the primary school-age population, the distribution is as follows:

China	34.3 per cent;
India	31.3 per cent;
Brazil	7.2 per cent;
Indonesia	6.6 per cent;
Pakistan	5.4 per cent;
Nigeria	5.1 per cent;
Bangladesh	5 per cent;
Mexico	3.4 per cent;
Egypt	1.9 per cent.

Estimates and projections of the official primary-school-age population according to national regulations in the E-9 countries suggest that :

The E-9 countries account for more than half (55%) of the world's primary-school-age population. This proportion remained unchanged over the past decade.

The average annual growth rate of the primary-school-age population in the period 2000-2010 is estimated as being negative (-0.47%) for the E-9 as a whole. This trends result from different country patterns. Although the growth rates are declining in all E-9 countries, they remain positive in Bangladesh, Egypt, Nigeria and Pakistan, while Brazil, China, India, Indonesia and Mexico are experiencing a negative growth rate of their school-age population.

In 2000, about 387 million or 12 per cent of the total E-9 population were in this age group. In 2010 the proportion will fall to 10 per cent and the number of primary-school-age children will decrease to 369 million. That means that the school-age population of the E-9 countries is moving at lesser pace than that of the rest of the world. The projected growth rate between 2000-2010 (-0.47%) is lower than that for the total population (1.2%) and is explained by the changing demographic structure, particularly in China, the biggest E-9 country.

These trends are mainly explained by the decline of the primary-school-age population in China and, to lesser degree, in India, Brazil, Indonesia and Mexico. For the remaining E-9 countries, the primary-school-age population will continue to increase during the period 2000-2010 but the growth will be lower than that observed in the past decade. Since the costs of providing UPE fall on the population of working age, a country's capacity to attain this goal depends directly on the school-age dependency ratio, i. e. the size of the school-age population in relation to the size of the active population. This ratio is declining in all the E-9 countries. Not surprisingly, the lowest ratio is found in China where the dependency ratio, stagnating around 13 per cent in 1990 and 2000, is expected to reach 9 per cent in 2010. In the 8 remaining countries, the burden of the primary-school-age population remains high, although the average for all the E-9 countries as whole is misleading owing to the weight of China.

Nevertheless, the fall in the school-age dependency ratio should facilitate the achievement of UPE, particularly in countries such as Bangladesh, India, Nigeria and Pakistan where sizeable portion of school-age children do not have access to school. For the remaining five countries where UPE is already a reality or near to being reached, the decline in the dependency ratio would make it possible to release resources that could help in improving the quality of education and/or in developing access to higher levels of education.

Adult illiteracy

In 2000 it was estimated that 71 per cent of the world's illiterate population, or 625 million adult illiterates, are in the E-9 countries. This share has remained almost constant since 1990, despite the decline recorded both in terms of the absolute number of illiterates and illiteracy rates. Currently, two of the E-9 countries, India and China, account for half of the world's illiterate population.

The alarming fact is the contrast between the E-9's contributions to these two parts of the adult population. It is striking to observe that the E-9 countries, which account for about 53 per cent of the world's adult population and 71 per cent of its adult illiterates, account for only 48 per cent of the world's adult literates. Although the adult illiteracy rate, or percentage of illiterates within the adult population, has constantly decreased over the decades, the E-9 countries taken as a whole still has a high proportion of adult illiterates, estimated at 27.7 per cent in 2000, as compared to the world average of 20.6 per cent and the average of 26.6 per cent for all the developing countries.

As is the case for other developing countries, the majority of adult illiterates in the E-9 countries are female. In 2000, women accounted for 64 per cent of total adult illiterates in the E-9 countries and this proportion has not changed since 1990.

The female illiteracy rate is estimated to be 36.2 per cent as compared to 19.4 per cent for men. The size of the current gender gap and the pace at which it has been narrowing over the past decade need particular attention and call for concrete actions to expand education for girls and women.

The E-9 countries taken as a whole have made visible progress in both raising the literacy rate and the number of literates, and also in reducing the number of illiterates. Between 1990-2000, the number of adult literates have increased from 1.2 million to 1.6 million (i. e.34% in relative terms) while the number of illiterates have declined slightly from 640 to 625 million (-2.4%). It would seem that literacy is growing faster among women than men in that the number of female literates increased by 41 per cent as compared to 30 per cent for male literates. By contrast, the number of male illiterates is decreasing faster (-4.5%) than that of female illiterates (-1.2%).

This global picture masks differences among countries as well as disparities within countries. With an average of 72 per cent adult literates in 2000, the estimated literacy rates in the E-9 countries range from a minimum of 41 per cent in Bangladesh to maximum of 91 per cent in China. In view of the assumption that progress towards full literacy becomes self- sustainable once a country reach a literacy rate of 70 per cent, the problem of illiteracy seems to be particularly serious for countries such as Bangladesh, Egypt, India, Nigeria and Pakistan. These countries have literacy rates of less than 70 per cent and, except Nigeria, they have experienced an increase in the number of adult illiterates over the past decade, the increase in the number of female illiterates being relatively more important than that of males.

For all remaining countries both the number of male and female illiterates decreased, and the decrease in the number of male illiterates was relatively more important than that of female illiterates, the exception being Brazil where the number of male illiterates shows slight increase. Brazil is also the only E-9 country where gender parity in literacy is a reality.

The divergent trends should not mask the fact that all the E-9 countries have experienced a consistent increase in their literacy rates over the past decades, for both men and women. Within countries the pace of reducing illiteracy differs widely between regions. The literacy profiles are characterized by strong urban/rural bias that often reflects and reproduces interregional socioeconomic disparities. Although data for rural/urban disparities are available for only three countries, it is evident that literacy rates for the rural areas are much lower than those for the urban areas.

The older the population, the higher the incidence of illiteracy with females remaining disadvantaged. For the E-9 countries as a whole, low average illiteracy rates of less than 20 per cent were observed among the 15-19 year olds in 1990, as against high illiteracy rates of more than 60 per cent among those aged 50 years and over. By 2000, the lowest illiteracy rates, i. e.15 per cent to 20 per cent, were common among the 15-34 years, while the average illiteracy rate of those aged 50 years and over fallen to round 50 per cent.

Although there was a decline in illiteracy rates across all age-groups, such reduction seems to be more important for older age-groups, i. e. those aged 30 years and over and who have the highest illiteracy rates. The lowest incidence of illiteracy found in the young age-groups is explained by the exposure of this population sub-group to the formal education system.

Primary education

All countries, except Pakistan, have established rules governing compulsory education, whose duration ranges from 5 years in Bangladesh to 9 years in China and Indonesia. Constitutions (legal texts) in most of these countries ensure the provision of compulsory and free primary education, at least in the public sector. Primary education lasts 5 years in Bangladesh, China, Egypt, India, and Pakistan; 8 years in Brazil and 6 years in the remaining E-9 countries. The entrance age to primary education is 5 years in Pakistan; 6 years in Bangladesh, Egypt, India, Mexico and Nigeria, and 7 years in Brazil, China and Indonesia. Most of these countries now have constitutional, legal or policy commitments making (declaring or encouraging) primary education free, compulsory and universal. But, since these commitments have not been translated into practise, UPE has not yet become a reality for some of the E-9 countries.

The E-9 countries account, altogether, for more than half of the world total enrolment in primary education. The proportion (56%) is almost the same as regarding the enrolled school-age children, i. e. those pupils who are eligible to be enrolled in primary school according to country regulations.

The E-9 contribution to the world's enrolled school-age population has steadily decreased over the past decade and this trends is expected to continue in the next fifteen years, at least. This trends can be explained by the changing demographic structure in most E-9 countries, and that of China in particular. In fact, due to the decline in their fertility rates, these countries have experienced a decrease in the shares of their school-age population while enrolments continue to increase, thus sustaining their progress towards UPE.

According to the results of EFA 2000 assessment, enrolment increased in all E-9 countries during the period 1990-98; the total number of pupils rose from 334.7 million to 383.3 million, representing a 14 per cent increase, and female enrolment, which made up 45 per cent of total enrolment in 1990 was 46 per cent in 1998.

The growth in total enrolment was higher than that of the primary-school-age population, resulting in an increasing enrolled proportion of this age-group, as measured by both gross enrolment ratio (GER) and net enrolment ratio (NER). As regards the UPE objective, one can consider that the E-9 countries, taken as a whole, have the capacity to enrol all school-age children as indicated by their GER that remained around 100 per cent during the period under observation (1990-98). But GER does not necessarily present the whole picture. Comparison between this global GER (98%) and NER (85%) suggests that sizeable portion of children above the official age for primary education are still in primary school. This can be explained by high repetition, late entrance or re-entrance after dropping-out.

The progress recorded during the decade can be more accurately measured through the evolution of the NER which increased from 78 per cent in 1990 to 85 per cent in 1998 for the E-9 countries as a whole. Taken individually, each country experienced a different trends concerning the progress towards UPE.

Currently, one can consider that the objective of UPE has already been reached or is close to attainment in China, Mexico, Brazil and Indonesia, and to lesser degree, in Egypt. These five countries have NERs above 90 per cent for 1998, i. e. more than 90 per cent of eligible children (those who should be in school) were enrolled. In spite of progress achieved in the remaining countries, their NERs are still below 80 per cent, except for Bangladesh. Also, despite progress achieved in girls' enrolment in all E-9 countries, globally the girls' NER remains lower than that of boys. The gender disparity is more accentuated in India, Nigeria and Pakistan; the remaining six countries are close to realizing parity between girls' and boys' enrolments.

The UPE objective, as re-affirmed in the Dakar Framework for Action, implies that all children enrol in and complete the primary school. Then, progress in NER, even where 100 per cent of the school-age group is enrolled, may not correspond to UPE, as in many countries pupils are likely to drop-out before completing the full cycle of primary education.

A variety of reasons (most of them linked to poverty) have been found as explanations to early drop-out from school. Among school determinants of this phenomenon, repetition is one of the most cited in different studies. The weight of drop-outs and repeaters affects the school internal efficiency, since it determines the holding power of a school system and its capacity to make pupils complete an education cycle in the prescribed length of time.

As far as EFA is concerned, the school survival rate to Grade 5 is of particular interest, since this level is commonly considered as pre-requisite for sustainable literacy. In this connection, available data showed that all the E-9 countries have recorded some progress as regards their school survival rates to Grade 5 over the past decade. In 1997/98, the rates were relatively high in China (90%), Indonesia (85%), Mexico (85%) and Egypt (96%).

Even though somewhat low compared to the above countries, the Bangladesh level of school retention has recorded notable improvement, increasing from 46 per cent in 1991 to 70 per cent in 1998. However, the level of early drop-out from primary school remains a serious concern for India and Pakistan where about half of the children who get enrolled in first class are at a risk to drop-out before reaching Grade 5.

To lesser degree, a high drop-out rate is also considered as one of the weaknesses of the Brazilian education system, whose the survival rate to the final year of primary education, Grade 8, was estimated at 66 per cent in 1997, a notable improvement as compared to

52 per cent in 1995. Early drop-out being more prevalent among male children and adolescents, the Brazilian Government has launched what it calls "minimum income programmes and actions "to fight child labour in order to address the issue and to ensure that all children attend school.

Some of the basic factors underlying low enrolment and high drop-out rates, include:

— poverty or economic hardship;

— child labour that raises the opportunity cost to send the child to school;

— distance from school;

— irrelevant curriculum and teaching-learning process;

— lack of facilities in schools;

— harsh attitude of certain teachers, particularly against female students;

— parental misunderstanding of the value of education; etc.

Depending on the individual country's priorities, different strategies have been adopted by particular countries to address these issues. Bangladesh has introduced Food For Education Programme (FFEP) with a built-in strategy to attract the poverty-stricken families to send their children to school, instead of engaging them for earning a livelihood.

The food given under the programme becomes the income entitlement to poor families and this enables them to release their children from livelihood obligations, and to enrol and retain them in primary schools. As a result, the drop-out rates of the programme schools are constantly decreasing (currently it is around 1%), as compared to those of non-programme schools (6%).

In order to raise the level of school retention, India has adopted a series of measures, including:

— incentive schemes such as free textbooks and uniforms, and attendance scholarships for children from socio-economically deprived sections;

— the Programme of Nutritional Support to Primary Education, popularly known as the Mid-day Meal Scheme, launched in 1995 on a nationwide basis, with the aim of enhancing UPE by increasing enrolment, retention and attendance, and improving the nutritional status of children in primary classes;

— encouraging separate girls' schools wherever necessary: special scholarships are provided to girls in several states, and education of girls is free at all levels, including university education; and the teacher recruitment procedure in almost all the states envisages that at least 50 per cent of the positions are filled by female teachers; and

— promotion of programmes for early childhood education (pre-school) and the creation of special residential schools known as ashram schools to accommodate children from nomadic groups and special ethnic communities living in remote hilly and forest areas. In addition to all these measures, improvement in teaching and learning materials and in pedagogic practices have received very high priority in DPEP as well as all other ongoing EFA projects.

The incidence of repetition has markedly decreased between 1990 and 1998 in the E-9 countries for which data are vailable. Despite this improvement, repetition continues to constitute a cause of inefficiency as well as an impediment to increasing access to primary education, especially for countries such as Brazil where the average repetition rate for the first five grades is still high, at about 15 per cent. This is the main cause of the age-grade gaps that have deeply affected the Brazilian education system in its entirety.

The age-grade gap caused by repetition has increased educational costs by about 30 per cent. Besides, the evaluations undertaken by INEP showed that the pupils who are delayed in their schooling career are likely to be affected as regards their self-esteem and performance. It was also stressed that these pupils tend to develop highly negative attitude toward school, leading to dropping out entirely.

The repetition rates observed in late 1990s in other E-9 countries seem relatively low (round 6 per cent in Bangladesh, Egypt, India, Indonesia and Pakistan; and 8 per cent in Mexico), as compared to those prevailing in most developing countries (round 16% for Sub-Saharan Africa, 13% for Latin America/Caribbean and 7% in southern Asia). China reduced its repetition rate from 6 per cent in 1990 to 0.9 per cent in 1998. In recent years, some Chinese local authorities have imposed a ceiling on repetition rates, and some even explicitly abolish grade repetition. But in Pakistan, where the policy of automatic promotion is practised up to Grade 3 in a number of schools, some parents and teachers have serious reservations, insisting that automatic promotion can further deteriorate the quality of education.

The size of the UPE challenge, as measured by both enrolment and school efficiency rates, remains high for the E-9 countries. In fact, despite their relatively high NERs, as compared to the average for all the developing countries, there are about 56 million school-age children not enrolled; this account for half of the world's out-of-school children. This shows clearly the magnitude of the effort needed to enrol all children in schools. The way in which the E-9 countries approach this challenge is of paramount interest as it affects world EFA trends.

Implications for EFA needs

The implications for EFA need to be assessed with reference to the two main goals:

— achievement of UPE by 2015 that represents the target for school-age children and;

— achievement of a 50 per cent improvement in the level of adult literacy by 2015.

The trends in enrolment and retention rates since 1990 suggest that, for the E-9 countries as a whole, the goal of UPE could be reached by 2015 if the current effort is maintained. However, the large socioeconomic differences between these countries do not allow an overall conclusion to be drawn concerning their paths towards UPE.

The global E-9 picture is heavily influenced by China's positive educational trends, masking the low level of educational development in countries such as Nigeria, Pakistan and Bangladesh. In the latter, more effort is needed to achieve UPE.

Table 4 provides a comparison between the past efforts (1990-98) towards UPE and the efforts required in the future to achieve UPE by 2015. Given the past trends

(1990-98), the remaining gap and, taking into account the demographic growth foreseen in the primary school-age population between 1998 and 2015, it is useful to compare the progress made between 1990 and 1998 (Jomtien effect)in expanding access to and cover age of primary education, to the efforts needed in 1998-2015 if the goal of enrolling all children of primary-school-age is to be attained (Dakar effect).

For six E-9 countries: Brazil, China, Egypt, India, Indonesia and Mexico, the pace required in enrolment increase to accommodate all school-age children by the year 2015 is lower than that observed in the period 1990-98. For Pakistan, the effort to increase enrolment would need to be made at relatively lower, but not negligible rate, while Bangladesh and Nigeria would need respectively the same rate and a substantially accelerated rhythm of enrolment increase to meet the UPE goals by 2015. These findings do not imply that the task of ensuring UPE would be necessarily easier than it was in the past decade, even for countries where UPE seems to require less efforts than in the past.

In general, the last 5 or 10 per cent out-of-school children are those from marginalized groups or isolated areas, the most difficult to reach. Also, this study did not take into account the qualitative aspects of EFA, in terms of learning achievement. In fact, while having all children enrolled and completing primary school is obviously an important priority, it is but the first step towards the goal of education for all. It doesn't ensure that the children received the quality instruction that will allow them to continue learning in an autonomous way.

Thus, in pursuing the efforts towards UPE, particular attention must be given to measurable learning achievement and outcomes rather than looking exclusively at enrolment numbers. This is also the way to ensure sustainable literacy skills and to accelerate the progress towards the EFA goals.

To achieve the literacy goal set by the World Education Forum, the E-9 countries, taken altogether, have to reduce their adult illiteracy rate from its current level of 28 per cent to about 14 per cent in 2015. In other words, the adult literacy rate should be 86 per cent by 2015. This implies that the number of adult literates have to increase annually by 56.7 million or total increase of 850.7 million, corresponding to 52.1 per cent increase from its current figure. Comparing to the progress made so far during the past decade, more efforts are required to meet the literacy goal set in Dakar. To meet the Dakar goals, the E-9 countries have to increase the effort by 1.3 times in general and by 1.4 for women.

The challenge is somewhat different for particular countries, as it can be seen in Table 5. While Brazil, China, Indonesia and Mexico could meet the Dakar literacy goal by maintaining almost the same efforts as in the past decade, more efforts are required for the remaining five E-9 countries. For Bangladesh and Pakistan, the future efforts required in increasing the number of adult literates should be more than two times the previous ones. Egypt and India would require about twice the previous efforts, while Nigeria would need to increase its efforts by 1.36 times. With exception of Brazil, the efforts required to meet the literacy goal would be relatively more important for women than for men.

For all the E-9 countries, the effort required to meet the literacy target is greater than that required for UPE. As the E-9 countries account for about 71 per cent of the world's illiterate population, it is clear that the struggle against illiteracy remains the main EFA challenge, especially for these nine countries.

In addition to UPE, which is the guarantee of the literacy skills for the young adults, more efforts are needed to develop adult and non-formal education so as to reach those children, youths and adults whose learning needs may not be adequately addressed by conventional or formal education. The magnitude of the task can be assessed using population and literacy pyramids showing in detail the literacy trends and distribution by sex and by age-group, within a changing demographic context. These figures indicate clearly the priority countries and target groups as regards age-group and sex, thereby contributing to the development of appropriate strategies to overcome illiteracy in particular countries. Lessons from different countries' experiences show how difficult it is to implement policies for the eradication of adult illiteracy.

To be effective, such policies require clear identification of priority target illiterate population which, depending on countries, could be a particular age-group, a disadvantaged group such as women, the disabled, rural or semi-urban poor, ethnic minorities or indigenous populations, etc. Hence, the educational or literacy approaches need to be tailored to specific economic and cultural contexts so as to be relevant and attractive for the potential learners.

The information and data presented here, in particular those related to literacy, re still based on rough estimates and should be interpreted with caution. Besides, the trends in literacy will be strongly influenced by the dynamics both in the development of primary education and in the ageing and mortality of the oldest age-groups in which are concentrated the majority of illiterate adults.

Country Experiences in non-formal education

Bangladesh

The following characteristics make non-formal education very effective in addressing the problem of large-scale adult illiteracy in Bangladesh:

— Non-formal education is meant to reach large numbers of people where they live and work; its objective is to impart useful knowledge and skill without removing people from their normal environment and responsibilities.

— Non-formal education is sufficiently diverse and enjoys adequate flexibility in organization, funding and management; it emphasizes local initiative, self-help and innovation on the part of large number of people and their local institutions; every successful learner can become in some degree a teacher.

— Non-formal education is designed to be able to pave its way through increased employment, productivity and social participation.

— Non-formal education makes learning a rational, lifelong learning experience, compatible with the interests of individuals and communities, for all economic levels of a society.

— Non-formal education encourages girls and women to take interest in improving their life situation.

Programmes and Ploicies

Considering the advantages of non-formal education in the struggle against adult illiteracy, especially the disparity between male and female illiteracy rates, the Government of Bangladesh has taken up programmes for non-formal education of children, adolescents and adults, with the following objectives.

Non-formal education programme

Objective: Provide a good quality basic education, through low-cost alternative channels, to those who were deprived of opportunities for formal schooling and to offer a second chance of learning to the school drop-outs.

Target groups :Children and adolescents 6-14 years

Estimated Population :1991 –14.7

(in millions)1995 –14.6

2000 –12.8

Coverage :1995 –11.9

(in millions)2000 –12.2

Cost :Takas 6,250 million

Programme for the reduction of the adult illiteracy rate

Objective :Provide illiterate adults, targeting women in particular, with opportunities for developing reading, writing and understanding skills as well as need-based functional/ vocational skills, and create opportunities for them to continue to learn.

Target groups :Population of 15-45 years.

Estimated population (in millions):

Year	Total	Female
1991	47.6	23.5
1995	52.9	26.1
2000	59.8	29.5

Coverage (in millions):

Year	Literates	Literacy(%)
1995	27.1	40
2000	46.9	62

Cost :

Adult education	Continuing education	Total cost (in million)
8 251	1100	9 351

The Government Programme to reduce the adult illiteracy rate has been incorporated in the National Plan for EFA and also in the fifth five-years plan (1997-2002) document.

Non-formal education programme for children and adolescents: Strategies for this programme include:

— Implementation of the government programmes for non-formal education through the Directorate of Non-formal Education.

— Earmark funds to provide subsidies for expanding non governmental organizations and community-level activities for literacy programmes.

— Encourage non-governmental organizations and other community-level organizations to draw up innovative programmes for literacy expansion at least cost.

— Assist community-level organizations and other non-government organizations to replicate successful models of integrated learning and other multi-sectoral development as well as skill generation for adults.

— Offer training facilities, monitoring and evaluation services and other technical assistance to non-government efforts.

— Prepare frameworks and guidelines for curricula and syllabuses for non-formal education to be followed by everyone as far as possible, without restricting innovations and piloting of models.

— Encourage Ministry of Social Welfare and other concerned government bodies to take up programmes of basic education for the handicapped and urge non-governmental organizations to undertake extensive programmes for the physically and mentally handicapped, and marginalized groups, and arrange material support for implementing these programmes.

Programme for reduction of adult illiteracy rate: Strategies for this programme include:

— Firm up the scope of work under the government project for Expansion of Integrated Non-Formal Education.

— Launch massive social mobilization and start a nation wide movement for eradication of illiteracy involving all concerned individuals in all communities.

— Prepare for establishing at least one literacy centre in each village by 1995 to be implemented by the local communities and the non-governmental organizations.

— Develop a model curriculum for the students of the adult literacy centres.

— Establish a National Academy for Non-Formal Education (NANFE), suitably staffed to conduct surveys, collect data, carry out research and evaluation, designing appropriate syllabuses for non-formal adult education, etc., and to provide necessary technical support to community-level non-governmental organizations initiatives for adult education.

— Establish a suitably staffed Directorate of Mass Education (DME) under the Ministry of Primary and Mass Education to administer the national mass literacy programmes. Assist community-level organization and non-governmental organizations as well as local government institutions, including the proposed Village Development Committees, to have access to the use of the national press, radio, television, etc., for advocacy and education as well as provide financial supports for developing and disseminating information on adult education and its contents through posters, cinema, slides, printed materials, folk arts, etc.

— Provide funds for the development and distribution of specially prepared extension materials for disseminating functional knowledge in agriculture, fisheries, livestock, horticulture, etc., written in simple language and illustrated with pictures.

— Provide financial support for establishing a small public library in each village equipped with suitable textbooks and reading materials.

— Institute suitable monitoring and evaluation system for the nationwide adult literacy activities, and provide for appropriate incentives and rewards for successful and innovative works in the field of adult literacy as well as for achieving outstanding results.

Achievements

Basic education for 6-14 age-group: Children and adolescents of the age-group 6-14 years were estimated at 12.2 million by 2000. The target for enrolment at basic Grade 1 has been set at 521,500. The gross enrolment has been found to be 149,000 under INFEP and 235,500 under NFE-3, making the total enrolment at 384,500 which is 73.7 per cent of the target.

Basic education enrolment for adults: Again, under the adult literacy programme, the target population of age-group 15-45 years was been estimated to be 49.9 million in 2000. The non-formal education programme under EFA has not covered the entire population of the relevant age groups. As it stands, the EFA target has been set at 1.14 million (INFEP),2.95 million under NFE-1,8.18 million under NFE-2 and 22.88 million under NFE-4 thereby making a total of 35.15 million adults. Thus, programmes have been undertaken to reach 70 per cent of the adult population, that is to say, those aged 15-45 years.

A review of the non-formal education programmes indicates that gross enrolment to basic education under these programmes has been 2 million under INFEP, 1.26 million under NFE-1, 3.34 million under NFE-2 and 4.19 million under NFE-4, a total of 10.8 million or 30.6 per cent of the target.

Contribution of NGOs to basic education: Non-governmental organizations' involvement in education followed from the Government decision to have non-governmental organizations complement government efforts towards universal primary education, in particular since the adoption of World Declaration on Education for All. Non-governmental organizations, community-based organizations (CBO), and private voluntary organizations (PVO) are engaged in offering non-formal basic education (NFBE) and non-formal primary education (NFPE). More specifically, the programmes are:

— Early childhood (pre-primary) education programme

— Non-formal basic/primary education programme for children (6-10 age-group)

— Non-formal basic education programme for adolescents (11-14 age-group)

— Non-formal basic education programme for adults (15-45 age-group)

The nationwide non-formal education programme is implemented under three delivery modes:

— Centre-Based Approach (CBA) through NGOs .

— Total Literacy Movement (TLM), through districts administration

— Primer distribution to PVOs and CBOs

CBA covers about 33 per cent of the total non-formal education programme and subventions are provided to non-governmental organizations that implement the programme. The remaining 67 per cent of the programme is implemented by the district administration under TLM approach through mobilizing local community. In addition to participating in government non-formal education programme, non-government organizations independently run NFBE programme.

In order to encourage the small voluntary organizations in providing NFE, the DNFE provides free primers and guidebook. According to list vailable from the Association of Development Agencies in Bangladesh (ADAB), there are 993 NGOs in the country of whom 418 offer non-formal education literacy programmes under a subvention programme from the government and 306 provide NFPE programmes. NGO's programmes are, however, mainly urban-based. Dhaka Division has the highest concentration of NGOs (47.4%) while Sylhet Division has the lowest concentration (3.7%). About 56.8 per cent of the total NGOs are located in urban areas and 65 per cent of the urban NGOs are concentrated in Dhaka Division.

The NGOs operate 121,135 basic education centres with an enrolment of 3.6 million. About 55 per cent of the enrolment are females. Each centre has on average one teacher and 30 learners. Male-female ratio of teachers is 45:55; urban-rural ratio of both enrolment and teacher is 6:94. On average, the number of basic education centres per NGO is 992 in Sylhet Division followed by Chittagong Division (600 per NGO). Rajshahi Division has 489 centres per NGO, while Dhaka Division has the lowest position with 172 centres per NGO.

Dhaka Division has the highest concentration of enrolment (33.9%) followed by Rajshahi Division (23.8%) and Chittagong Division (20.31%). Barisal Division has the lowest enrolment concentration (3.65%). About 31 per cent (306) NGOs are involved in NFPE programmes and a great majority of learning centres (93%) and enrolment (92%) are located in Dhaka Division, particularly in urban areas of Dhaka Division (89%). There re 38,288 NFP schools with an enrolment of 1,342,362 of whom 63 percent are girls. The number of teachers in the non-formal primary schools stands at 40,347.

The gross enrolment ratio (GER) for non-formal basic education programme works out to be 10.6 per cent (based on total enrolment under non-formal basic education through centre-based approach. Under the NFPE programme GER is 7.1 per cent as against 96.5 per cent at the formal primary education level. This is based on a total enrolment in NFPE of 1.34 million and a total primary-school-age population of 19 million.

Brazil

Since the establishment of Brazilian Republic, the illiteracy issue has been mobilized by Brazilian intellectual leaders. Since the end of the nineteenth century, educators, politicians and journalists have been decrying the high illiteracy rates prevailing in the country as a national shame and demanding strong actions from the Government to eradicate this evil from the Brazilian society. It is in this context that the programmes for youth and adult education, the so-called EJA, have been promoted. Until recently, youth and adult education was relegated to secondary position in the general framework of educational policies in Brazil. It was regarded as compensatory offering " second chance " to those who had been unable to attend school at the proper age. Because youth and adult education concerned the schooling of people who belonged mostly to the poorest segments of society, EJA was never fully integrated into a national project for education.

In the late 1980s and early 1990s, several studies stressed the need for EJA to become part of specific policy devised and planned around the universe of young people and working adults. This process of progressive recognition of the importance and specific nature of adolescents and adults bore relevant results. The first of these was the inclusion in the Constitution of 1988, of the guarantee of compulsory and free primary education, even for those who have not had access to it at the proper age. This constitutional provision was later changed with the elimination of the compulsory nature of education for adolescents and adults but the duty remained for the State to provide it free of charge.

Programmes and Policies

The Education Guidelines and Framework Law of 1996 included new ideas regarding EJA, based on the acknowledge that attention had to be paid to the needs and interests of those individuals who already have certain experience in life and are part of the labour force, and who therefore possess quite different background from the children and adolescents who form the target audience of regular primary education. So EJA came to occupy prominent position amid what is usually called "continuing, lifelong education ".

Data relating to illiteracy in Brazil show the population without or with less than one year of schooling highly concentrated in the age-group above 40 years, and especially over 60. Notwithstanding, the situation of the younger age groups is no less worrisome.

The portion of children aged between 10 and 14 without or with less than one year of schooling totals

10.1 per cent, double the figure registered for young people between 15 and 19 years old –5.4 per cent. In the latter age-group, however, 21.7 per cent of the adolescents failed to complete the first 4 grades and 66.6 per cent have not completed the 8 years of primary education. The indices for the age-group of 20-24 are better, thus confirming the phenomenon of late schooling and backwardness due to repetition: 20.1 per cent failed to conclude the 4 first grades and 55.9 per cent did not complete the basic 8 years of school.

The regional concentration of illiteracy is another feature of this problem, which reflects and reproduces interregnal socioeconomic inequalities. In the 1990s, the pace of decline in illiteracy rates was not the same, although the trend can be perceived in all regions of the country.

The illiteracy rate among adolescents aged 15-19 dropped from 12.1% in 1991 to 6% in 1996. Similar results were registered for individuals in the 20-24 age-group, whose illiteracy rate fell from 12.2% to 7.1% over the same period. For the group aged 25-29, a trend toward rapid decline in the illiteracy rate has also been observed.

As a result of expansion of programmes for the education of youths and adults, illiteracy rates are falling rapidly and the average schooling of the population has tended to increase. Between 1990 and 1996, average schooling years rose from 5.4 to 5.7 among the male population and from 4.9 to 6.0 among women.

Brazil has made great efforts towards the education of the adult population aged 15 or over. The School Census for 1998 shows the magnitude of this effort, despite the fact that the data collected concerns only programmes for which the teachers were evaluated

Numerous programmes offered, especially by NGOs, were therefore not included in the Census.

A total of 2.88 million Brazilians are enrolled in these school-based courses, most of whom are completing their primary education. Enrolment in the upper grades is higher than in the first grades, which is positive factor in that it shows that they have already completed that level of schooling. The number of students in secondary education, also included in this section, amounts to about 18 per cent of the whole and indicates the population's effort to achieve a more advanced level of schooling. Unfortunately, the vocational training courses computed in the first two columns, and which would be the most suitable for this population, are still very few in number, totalling less than 5 per cent of all enrolments.

The supply of primary education by far surpasses the literacy courses, which are being replaced by programmes of broader scope. The data per age group confirm the effort to make up, albeit belatedly, for deficient schooling: over two-thirds of the population enrolled in these courses are over 18 years of age.

School-based courses are predominantly public. The private sector, including the courses offered by NGOs, covers no more than 12.7% of enrolments.

Achivements

In spite of the significant progress made through the decade, the main difficulty of EJA policies in Brazil is still the precarious service that fails to satisfy the existing potential demand. The fact that this educational programme has been mostly covering the youth population is yet another reason for the Federal

Administration to raise investments in the are and ensure access to education to citizens with a great contribution to give to the country in economic, social, political and cultural terms.

Accordingly, EJA policies for the decade to come have to face great challenges: increase vailable resources, expand the coverage, strengthen the qualification and permanent training of teachers, adjust programs to the concept of continuing education, with special emphasis on the needs related to the labour market and strengthening of citizenship, integration with cultural and sports activities, and promoting access to information and new technologies. One must recognize, however, that while the faster drop registered in the illiteracy rate is positive factor, the illiteracy rate of 14.7 per cent is still too high and represents, in absolute figures, over 15.5 million individuals. In defining a policy to reduce illiteracy rates more rapidly, policy-makers must take into account the fact that the phenomenon does not affect the population uniformly.

China

Since its establishment, the People's Republic of China (PRC), has adopted a policy of opening the door to workers and peasants in education and regarded literacy work among them as an important function of the government. Accordingly the Government Administration Council set up Committee for Workers' and Peasants' Education, which undertook to organize literacy education among urban workers and mass literacy campaigns during the slack winter seasons among peasants.

By 1964 the illiteracy rate of the population was reduced to 54.8 per cent from 80 per cent at the time of the founding of the PRC. By 1982, the illiteracy rate of the entire population of China was reduced to 22.8 per cent, and by 1990, this figure was reduced to 15.9 per cent. China has the biggest population in the world, and in 1990 China's illiterate and semiliterate population was still as high as 180 million, accounting for nearly one fifth of the world's total illiterate population. By 1998, the number of adult illiterates aged 15 and above had dropped to 135 million and the number of young and middle-aged illiterates dropped to 30 million, the literacy rate of the young and middle-aged population reached 94.5 per cent. Illiteracy had been eliminated among the young and middle-aged population in over 2,500 counties and 25 provinces and municipalities.

Whether we can reduce the illiteracy rates as soon as possible and raise the educational attainment of the people is not only a grim challenge we have to face in order to facilitate economic and social development in the poor areas, to improve the socioeconomic status of these illiterate people, and to enhance their participation in political life as citizens, but also an undertaking which affects to large extent the timely and effective attainment of the goals set by WCEFA. To meet the learning needs of adults in China, a relatively independent subsystem of adult education has been set up as an integral part of the education system of China.

Programmes and Policies

Adult education may be divided into three categories in the light of the specific features of adult learners and the nature of adult education:

— post-literacy education: its purpose is to consolidate the gains of literacy work and prevent relapse into illiteracy, and to enable the neo-literates to survive and live better, and to improve their employ - ability;

— vocational/skills training for adults: its purpose is to help adults to adapt to the needs of the world of work and acquire job-related skills. This kind of training has a very broad scope, and its target groups include both the neo-literate and those with higher educational attainment; and the training programs provided include both pre-employment training and in-service training and training for job transfer;

— formal or quasi-formal adult education for the acquisition of formal academic qualifications: its purpose is to provide compensatory education for adults who were deprived of the opportunity of formal schooling or dropped out before completion of their schooling.

The first and second categories of adult education are mainly provided by adult primary and secondary schools, vocational training schools/centres, secondary vocational schools, and training courses run by NGOs, enterprises and institutions. The third category of adult education is mainly provided by adult primary and secondary schools and adult higher education institutions.

In order to further reduce the illiteracy rates and enhance the educational attainment of the nation, the Chinese government has placed literacy work as one of the priorities in educational development, and accordingly set targets to be attained by the end of the century:

— As specific target, by 2000, illiteracy should be eliminated among the young and middle-aged population aged 15-50 in areas inhabited by 90 per cent of the country's total population and the literacy rate of the young and middle-aged population should reach 95 per cent. On an average, 4 million illiterates (of whom 3 million are females) should become literate annually. Great attention and support should be given to education for national minorities and education for the disabled, so that compulsory education can be implemented among the normal and disabled children simultaneously.

— Rural adult education should be energetically developed by running well the existing cultural and technical schools for adults in rural towns and townships, and by proper integration of cultural education with vocational training in an endeavour to raise the quality of the rural work.

In order to attain the above objectives/targets and in order to fulfil China's commitment to WCEFA and concerned IGOs, the Chinese government has placed literacy work as one of the priorities in educational development, and accordingly has taken more important and effective measures. Following is an account of the strategies adopted:

— Subsequent to the promulgation of the Regulations on Eradicating Illiteracy by the State Council on 5 February 1988, SEDC issued suggestions on further strengthening literacy work in October 1991, and the State Council issued the revised version of the Regulations on Eradicating Illiteracy. The more important revisions are related to the age cohort of the priority target group, criteria set for literacy standards to be attained by the neo-literate, and explicit requirements concerning the rights and obligations of the illiterate to receive education.

— At the national level an Interdepartmental Coordination Group should be set up to coordinate the efforts of various departments and quarters concerned, with suitable division of responsibilities. At the provincial, prefectural and county levels, similar bodies should also be set up. These bodies are required to convene meetings regularly to discuss relevant matters and coordinate the plans formulated and measures taken by various departments and NGOs concerned in an endeavour to push forward the work of all concerned.

— Instituting a system of verification and acceptance of literacy work. The responsibilities of the acceptance exercise mainly lie with the bodies of educational inspection and the bodies in charge of literacy work among adults. As a rule it is conducted in a county-level administrative unit following the sequence: universalizing primary education –basically eradicating illiteracy –basically universalizing 9-year compulsory schooling. The main procedures are as follows: Once the achievement in all townships and towns under its jurisdiction have met the requirements for acceptance, the county government submit the result to the provincial-level government over it, subject to confirmation by the provincial-level government through process of sample checks. Once the results are confirmed by the provincial-level government, the final result is reported to the national educational department, subject to its confirmation through a process of verification through sample checks. Then a list of all the qualified counties is published in national papers. By the end of 1998 the number of counties, cities and districts having satisfactorily passes such acceptance reached 2,400, accounting for nearly 80 per cent of the number of county-level units in the whole country, and 24 provinces and municipalities have passed the acceptance of basically eradicating illiteracy among young and middle-aged adults.

— Implementing a system of commendation and rewards. There are three categories of rewards in operation. The first category of reward is conferred by Ministry of education or by Ministry of education and Ministry of finance jointly to provinces and municipalities outstanding in literacy work. In 1991,18 provinces and municipalities were given varying monetary rewards for their outstanding achievements in literacy work; and in 1994 and 1995 Jilin Province and Heilongjiang Province were granted each a monetary reward of 1 million Yuan for basically eradicating illiteracy among young and middle-aged adults. In 1996 the People's Governments of Jiangsu, Guangdong, Shandong, and Anhui were cited for their outstanding achievements in literacy work. The second is to give SEDC-sponsored commendations to outstanding units and individuals. In the five consecutive years 1992-1996,276 advanced units, 300 outstanding individuals, and 419 advanced schools were commanded by SEDC. Mr Du Yijin, Deputy Governor of Anhui Province was warded the honorary "Zhonghua Literacy Prize ",10 advanced individuals were awarded special grade "Zhonghua Literacy Prizes ", and 189 individuals and 98 educational units were awarded "Zhonghua Literacy Prizes ". The third category is the "Women's Literacy Awards "jointly granted by ACWF and SEDC (MOE)with a view to promoting literacy work among women. In 1991,1994 and 1995 altogether 90 advanced units and 392 advanced individuals were winners of the "Women's Literacy Awards ".

The state has taken a series of measures to guarantee the conditions for literacy work, and following is a brief account of these measures:

— Implementing bodies –the main sites used for conducting literacy education include the literacy classes affiliated to rural primary schools, as well as the evening schools of regular primary schools and literacy classes run by township cultural centres.

— The literacy teachers are mainly part-time, with a small number of full-time teachers mainly employed in the primary schools for peasants (numbering 45,000 in 1998). The part-time teachers consist mainly of the full-time teachers of rural primary schools and other staff members and higher-grade pupils.

— With regard to the financing of literacy work, the Regulations on Eradicating Illiteracy promulgated by the State Council lists the following five venues:

  — funds raised by the governments of townships and towns, by urban neighbourhoods and by councils of villagers;

  — literacy work conducted in enterprises and institutions may be financed by budgetary allocations earmarked for the education of staff and workers;

  — part of the educational surcharges collected on certain taxes in rural areas;

— the expenses of training teachers and full-time literacy workers, of compiling teaching materials, of research activities, of experiences exchange and of commendation and rewards may be defrayed by funds of the educational budget;

— donations made by various NGOs and individuals.

In 1995 SEDC issued a circular, which further clarifies that earmarked funds for rewarding outstanding units and individuals of literacy work may be defrayed with budgetary appropriations;in localities where projects of supporting compulsory education in poor areas are being carried out, funds for literacy work may be defrayed with local matching funds for the project

— *Literacy textbooks*: In order to ensure that literacy work meets local needs, and is effectively integrated with the needs of economic development of the rural areas, with the needs of alleviating poverty and helping local people to get prosperous, the state's educational department has explicitly emphasized that textbooks used for literacy work should be compiled by local authorities with reference to the state's requirements in the light of local conditions.

Achievements

In China during 1991-97, the number of primary schools for adults increased from 110,500 to 140,800, while the number of literacy classes decreased from 358,800 to 283,000. The annual average output of neo-literates per school decreased from 480 to 286, and the average size of each class decreased slightly from 14.7 to 14.3. The total output of these primary schools for adults during these seven years amounts to 33.7 million indicating that an average of 4.8 million illiterate adults became literate every year, well over the target figure of 4 million per year set by the state. In the same period, China's adult population aged 15 and over increased from 813 million to 947 million. With effective progress in literacy education, the illiterate adult population decreased from 182 million to 153 million, a reduction of 18.8 per cent.

There are two noteworthy phenomena related to these changes in illiterate population.

— From 1993 onward, the number of neo-literates tends to decline gradually. There are three contributing factors:

  a) with the progress of literacy work, the weight of young and middle-aged adults has declined;

  b) eradicating illiteracy among the remaining illiterates has become all the more difficult;

  c) some of the areas which have passed the acceptance exercise related to eradication of illiteracy, relaxed their efforts in literacy work.

— The weight of female illiterates increased instead of declining. In 1990 female illiterates account for 67.9 per cent of total illiterate adults, and this figure increased to 71.4 per cent, indicating an increase of 4.5 percentage points.

This phenomenon can be explained as follows. Besides the slight increase of weight of females among young and middle-aged adults, the main cause is that among the neo-literates, the weight of females is lower than the weight of females in the total population. In the years with vailable data, the former is invariably lower than the latter. This phenomenon indicates that although the state has accorded high priority to literacy work among women, as evidenced by the number of official documents related to this issue, and the large amount of work done, the excessively high weight of female illiterates has not been altered yet. Still more effective measures are needed to intensify the literacy work among women.

It is an extremely arduous task to implement education for all in an all round way, eliminate the remaining illiteracy, and consolidate and improve what has been achieved. It was not possible to universalize 9-year compulsory education by the end of the twentieth century in poor areas inhabited by 15 per cent of the country's total population.

As economic development has been slow in these areas, educational input is far from enough and conditions for running schools are generally poor; few teachers can be assigned to these areas and they will not stay even if they are assigned there. As a result, there is distinct disparity in terms of overall quality of teachers between these areas and those that are more developed economically, and achievement of education for all is extremely difficult. The absolute number of illiterates is high and China is still one of the countries with a large illiterate population. The remaining illiterates mainly live in poor areas, border regions and national minority areas. They are scattered and it is getting more and more difficult to organize them for literacy programmes. As for the areas that have been checked and accepted for universalization of 9-year compulsory education and elimination of illiteracy, what has been achieved is only the minimum requirements, and inevitably the standards are low, the foundations weak and the indicators keep fluctuating.

Development is uneven from are to area. It will be a protracted and arduous task to consolidate what has been achieved and raise the overall quality in the universalization of 9-year compulsory education and elimination of illiteracy. The contradiction between the development of education for all and lack of funds is still very pressing. As education for all develops in scope, educational input is getting insufficient. In most areas, education for all is funded by county and township fiscal administrations. In some areas, township revenue is very scanty and many rural schools have great difficulty in finding the funds they need to keep the school going.

Egypt

In Egypt Law No.8 was issued in 1991 for literacy and adult education with the aim of mobilizing efforts for the organization of the comprehensive national campaign. The law stipulated the establishment of the General Organization of Literacy and Adult Education in 1992. The Organization started carrying out the various planning responsibilities as well as the executive, educational and coordinating efforts among different institutions involved in the implementation of the National Plan of Literacy and Adult Education scheduled for the decade (1992-2001) through its branches in 26 governorates in 251 educational idaras, covering 1,047 main villages and 20,945 hamlets.

In 1989 President Mubarak declared the 1990s a National Decade for Literacy and Adult Education. He also declared that literacy, for the remaining illiterates, is an urgent and essential objective for realizing development and increasing production. Hence, it is important to enhance and mobilize all national potentials for the eradication of illiteracy by the beginning of the new century.

The number of illiterates in rural areas is more than double their number in urban areas. For this reason, the Ministry of Education, in addition to the General Organization of Literacy, is making major efforts to eradicate illiteracy in rural areas and the places deprived of educational services. According to the 1996's population figures, the national illiteracy rate stands at 38.6 per cent. The gender disparity were very pronounced, with a female illiteracy rate of 50.2 per cent, as compared to 29 per cent for males. In 1999, the illiteracy rates were reduced to 45 per cent for females and 24 per cent for males, maintaining an unchanged gender gap of about 21 percentage points.

Bearing in mind the targets of the National Campaign for Literacy and Adult Education, and considering the directions addressed by the Minister of Education in his book Education and the Future, the main objectives of literacy in Egypt are recognized as follows: Providing illiterates with the basic skills of reading, writing and arithmetic that enable them cope with the professional levels of the various institutions and participate in the different fields of comprehensive development. In addition, they are provided with necessary skills and experiences for vocational fields as well as the basic knowledge included in the different subjects of primary education.

Among other objectives of literacy are reviving and emphasizing the traditional social trends of the Egyptians and intensifying their application through various every day life activities, while formulating sound attitudes towards continuing education and self-learning skills. Illiterates are supposed to reach the level of primary education certificates as a compulsory stage from where they can proceed to the higher educational stages.

The National Plan of Literacy targeted illiterates aged 15 to 35 years up to December 1998:

— Number of targeted illiterates: 6.2 million

— Number of enrolments in literacy classes: 3.8 million

— Percentage of the enrolled illiterates compared to the targeted numbers: 61 per cent

Illiterates who are above 35 years old are left free to choose either to be educated or not, while giving priorities to the most deprived categories (females –poor people –dwellers of rural and remote areas, etc).

Programmes and Policies

The General Organization of Literacy and Adult Education tended to utilize modern methods to confront the problem of non-enrolment in literacy classes or dropping-out. It has used several untraditional innovative educational methods, besides providing the official normal literacy classes. They are :

— Voluntary literacy programmes through free contracts with undergraduate teachers from the colleges of education, graduates of university colleges and institutes, and clergymen who are requested to educate illiterates. The organization provide the books and the necessary teaching aids without any charges. After a period of at least six months, illiterates are tested and are warded promotion certificates. The educators are given bonuses and incentives. The programme of voluntary literacy through free contracts has been executed lately with 5,000 contractors helping 100,000 persons become literates.

— Organization of mobile educational car vans for villages and remote areas in which thinkers and intellectuals participate to raise awareness on the importance of literacy and encourage illiterates to join the classes: 400 car vans were sent to villages and hamlets.

— Inviting businessmen to combat illiteracy of the citizens of their villages, through establishment of a complex including educational, vocational, cultural, health and sport centres, as a kind of social investment in their societies.

— Use of the television channels and broadcasting as a teaching aid for distance education.

— Preparation for receiving the transmission of the thematic Nile Sat literacy educational channel.

— Supporting and generalizing the pilot experiences of NGOs in literacy and adult education fields, to maximize the role played by community participation in literacy fields.

— Encouraging self-learning through recording literacy lessons on tapes and distributing them free with literacy books.

— Printing Braille literacy books to serve blind illiterates.

— The establishment of multi-purpose centres for literacy, vocational training, library, kindergarten and health care.

— Opening literacy classes in prisons, orphanages, health units, women clubs, accommodation institutions, worship institutions, youth centres, public clubs and even in homes.

— Study is conducted at times suitable for the students. Teachers are provided. Notebooks and educational aids are distributed freely.

— Preparation and qualification of 121,758 literacy class teachers during the period 1993-99; the total number of supervisors and inspectors amounted to 7,630 trainees.

— Using new encouraging catch words such as the "educated village " and the "educated family "to encourage self-learning.

— Pioneer women, as well as the educated women, and agricultural and health care guides are asked to help eradicate the illiteracy of rural women.

Other innovative actions have also been undertaken in the fields of curricula development, of evaluation and assessment of performance, of co-operation and co-ordination between the Organization and the various institutions participating in the efforts of literacy and adult education. In order to enhance linkages between literacy programmes and vocational training to provide illiterates with vocational skills, the Organization provides them with training for some handicrafts, according to their individual abilities and desires, with the aim of increasing production and improving the living standard of the families.

Achivements

Illiteracy rates were reduced from 49.4 per cent in 1986 to 38.6 per cent in 1996, i. e a reduction of 10.8 percentage points. The illiteracy rate further declined to 34,2 per cent, according to the 1999 assessment. This is a major achievement, particularly when considered in the light of the adopted policy of comprehensive economic reform.

The Ministry is trying to achieve faster rates for reducing these numbers by the end of the Literacy Decade (2001/2002). Because the numbers of female illiterates in rural areas amount the double of their numbers in the urban areas, the Ministry is providing One-Class Schools for girls aged 8-14 years to raise the female literacy rates in the country side.

Numbers of female illiterates reached 10.3 million according to 1996 statistics, numbering 6.9 million in the rural areas (67.1%)and 3.5 million in the urban areas (32.9%). According to 1998/99 statistics, the proportion of female enrolment has increased to 72 per cent of the total number of enrolment in literacy classes. This should imply an improvement in literacy gender parity index.

The previous numbers prove that, despite social and economic constraints which impede the illiterates enrolment in literacy classes, great improvement has been achieved showing thc increase in their access to these classes. It has also been indicated that number of illiterate females exceed that of the males.

Reading indicators prove that illiteracy rates are rapidly reduced in younger age-group than in the older ones, confirming the efficiency of the educational policy in expanding access to education. They also indicate the effectiveness of literacy programmes for the adults, since the adult literacy rate is estimated at 66 per cent in 1999, as compared to 53 per cent in 1990. However, these national figures mask a wide gender gap in literacy.

During five years of the plan the number of illiterates enrolled in literacy classes have reached 2 million, while they reached 1.8 million only during the next two years. These figures demonstrate the magnitude of the efforts made by the government and the positive response of the users towards the National Plan for Literacy and Adult Education.

Investment on Information Media for Illiteracy is one of a major qualitative achievement in the struggle against illiteracy. An information media campaign has been organized with the aim of inviting and urging the people to participate in combating illiteracy. Several activities have been carried out in this regard. The most important are the following:

— TV items to acquaint and urge illiterates get enrolled in literacy classes. Local TV channels transmit literacy lessons through different periods in order to give them an opportunity to follow these programmes according to their conditions and circumstances. Information material on the National Campaign of Literacy are transmitted in the different local and central broadcasting networks. Newspapers and media cover age high-light the activities undertaken by the Organization and its affiliated centres in the governorates.

— Sixty drama episodes have been transmitted on the literacy lessons (learn and get enlightened).

The Organization has also established a special department for post-literacy in order to ensure the fulfilment of life long, continuous education, and to find better conditions for post-literates and prevent their relapse into illiteracy. While ensuring the utilization of acquired skills and knowledge, the Organization encourages them to continue their progress through the preparatory education (the second stage of basic education).

The age of enrolment in the first preparatory grade has been raised to eighteen years old. By 1997 about 9,935 were enrolled in the preparatory stage. During the period 1997 to 1999 the number of illiterates joining literacy classes are 36,149. In 1997, a newspaper called "Enlightenment " was issued for distribution among classes and centres of literacy and among post-literates. Besides, one hundred libraries for post literate reading materials have been established in the governorates in order to encourage Reading for All.

The special department for post literates, instituted in different governorates, organizes training courses forateaching English language, computer and word processing. Other training courses for women are also held to raise awareness of the female post-literates and allow them to continue their education. Special project management courses are offered with the aim of promoting the skills of new post-literates.

The Organization has scheduled to complete an integrated system of information and support of decision making during 1999. This system was projected to link the central information system of the Organization with its affiliated centres in the governorates through a network of computers thereby creating a database on the numbers of illiterates and programme beneficiaries. The social Fund for Development supports the governorate officer with computers according to a set plan. It was also planned to connect the system with internet in order to provide global information in the field of literacy and adult education.

Future plans

The General Organization of Literacy and Adult Education is scheduling future plans for eradicating illiteracy for the rest of illiterates who are 15-35 years old, the drop-outs and those who failed in getting the literacy certificate within the period of the three years, through educating them in four educational courses of 9 months each. The main features of these plans include:

— Coordination among participating institutions should be realized in order to keep the aforementioned schedules.

— Literacy should always be connected with vocational training with the aim of raising the social standard of poor families.

— Local and executive institutions should be involved in publicizing the importance of literacy programmes. Country leaders, rural educated people and agricultural guides should take part in these efforts in order to finish this campaign according to the scheduled plan. Continuous education for all through the different stages of life should be encouraged. Establishing a department for special education for the deaf within the General Organization of Literacy and Adult Education, responsible for developing and improving curricula meet the educational requirements of the deaf, while stressing the importance of preparing a teacher manual for educating the illiterate deaf persons to enable them improve these programmes.

— Making use of the educational broadcasting channels dedicated to combating illiteracy and disseminating through Egyptian Nil-Sat when it begins its programs in literacy, adult education fields, teacher training and launching campaigns in the context of the literacy national campaign.

— Inviting educated women to participate in literacy voluntary projects (the educated woman teaches the uneducated woman) in their families, communities and villages. Encouraging the setting up of women's societies to work as the core of a women's Egyptian Union for Literacy.

— Establishing reading clubs for new literates and more and better libraries.

India

Adult education and literacy programmes have been transformed under the auspices of the National Literacy Mission (NLM) into a mass campaign leading towards a people's movement for total literacy and a new awakening for education. The goal of NLM is to attain full literacy (i. e., the sustainable threshold level of 75%). To achieve this goal, NLM is focusing on functional literacy for illiterates in the 15-35 age-group. This age-group was selected because it corresponds to the productive and the reproductive period of life.

NLM seeks to bring illiterates to a level of self-reliance in the three R's. It also provides facilities for skills development in order to improve their economic status and well-being. It enables them to acquire values of national integration, environmental conservation, women's empowerment and family planning. And finally, it facilitates their participation in the development process. Functional literacy, encompassing all of the above, is the over all goal of NLM.

The campaign's success in the Ernakulam district of Kerala laid the foundations of the campaign approach. While developing a national strategy for the country, NLM was fully ware of the need for a diversity of approaches, given the regional variations in the country. It was also ware that, in many areas, participation of women and disadvantaged sections would require an intensive environment-building process. In this context, NLM efforts represent a major initiative for bringing together civil society to participate actively in popular movement for achieving literacy within a given timeframe.

Recognizing the fragile nature of literacy levels achieved through a campaign and the need to create a learning society, NLM provides for a post-literacy campaign to consolidate acquisition of literacy and to link learning skills with life skills. Similarly, in order to sustain the learning process in the community, NLM supports the establishment of continuing education centres that provide a package of life-linked services for neo-literates.

Programmes and Policies

The educational needs of out-of-school children are addressed through of non-formal education. In fact, despite considerable expansion of schooling facilities, a large segment of children from marginalized groups continues to be deprived of primary-school education. Recognizing the need for offering alternate means of providing primary education to such children, a progamme of non-formal education was launched by the government nearly two decades ago. This programme targets children aged 6-14 years who remain outside the formal system of education for variety of reasons. These include drop-outs from the formal schools, children from areas where there are no schools, children who assist in performing domestic chores such as fetching fuel, fodder, water, attending to siblings, grazing cattle, etc. and girls who are unable to ttend formal schools. The programme was revised and strengthened during the 1990s. Though the original scheme was meant only fourteen educationally backward states, it has been extended to cover urban slums, hilly, tribal and desert areas, and projects for working children in other states.

The non-formal education programme is characterized by flexibility that makes it easier to provide basic education to traditionally disadvantaged sections of population. Some of its important features are:

— condensed course of about two years' duration for lower primary and three years for upper primary level;

— part-time instruction at time and place convenient to learners in small groups;

— the village community provides the space and other facilities for running the centres;

— part-time instructor/supervisor locally recruited and trained;

— emphasis on flexibility and decentralization of management;

— use of curriculum and teaching-learning materials comparable to the formal system, and relevant to local environment and learners' needs; and

— testing and certification of students enable their entry into formal system.

The goals of EFA in India, as viewed in relation to the World Declaration on EFA, include:

— access to basic education for the unreached segments and uncovered habitations;

— qualitative improvement in content and processes of education to make them more responsive to learning needs of individuals –children, youth and adults, families, community and development in different sectors of social and economic life;

— consolidation and newer orientation wherever required in different areas of education through innovative programmes and changed role of educational personnel;

— community participation in education: making education a people's movement;

— evolving effective and efficient management structures in education.

With regard to adult education and non-formal education, it is expected that literacy and continuing education will continue to receive increased attention so as to achieve the goal of complete eradication of illiteracy in the age group 15-35 years and to enable the neo-literate to retain, improve and apply the newly acquired literacy skills to improve their quality of life.

Emphasis will be on consolidation and sustaining the adult education processes through increased participation of NGOs, panchayati raj institutions, youth organizations, teachers and student volunteers. The focus of the adult education programmes will be two-fold. While the post-literacy and continuing education needs of the neo-literates will be assured through opportunities for self-directed learning, equivalency programmes based on open schooling, job-oriented vocational education and skill-development programmes, a fresh momentum will be given to basic literacy programmes. This is essential in order to take care of the backlog of non-literates, including the dropouts and left-outs of the literacy campaigns and the out-of-school children who are at risk to join the adult illiterate population.

The main features of the approach adopted for planning and implementing EFA programmes (including adult and NFE) are:

a) *Holistic Approach* :characterized by

— a holistic view of basic education with greater linkages and integration between preschool, primary education, non-formal education and adult education;

— relating programmes of education with national concerns such as nutrition and health care, environment, small family norm and life skills education;

— collaboration of different departments and sectors of development with primary education.

b) *Decentralization: this* has been one of the major strategies for designing different programmes for

EFA and implementing them. Operationally, this can be characterized in terms of:

— shift from taking 'state' as the unit of planning to 'district' as the unit for programmes of basic education; and to move further to 'sub-district ' levels wherever found necessary and feasible;

— increasing community involvement in implementation and monitoring of programmes, and;

— participation of panchayati raj institutions (local self-government bodies in rural areas) and urban local bodies in planning and management of education.

— *Improved access for the deprived sections* :to ensure full accessibility not only in terms of availability of school but also in terms of facilitating conditions for participation of children.

— *Advocacy, campaign approach and mission mode* :in order to reach the common stake-holders, mass campaigns have been launched for creating awareness about educational needs of children, youth and adults, and help them to develop proper appreciation of the role of education in improving the quality of life. It is also evident that programmes in basic education have to be implemented in a mission mode involving the community in an effective manner through mechanisms such as District Literacy Committees, Village Education Committees and P rent-Teacher Associations. Literacy campaigns have made big strides in this direction and efforts are on to implement other basic education programmes in mission mode.

— *Legislative measures* :a significant change in the perspective towards basic education is that it is not viewed merely as a service provided by the state but as a right of every individual. The Supreme Court of India has recognized education as a fundamental right flowing from the right to life and liberty. It is with this in view that attempts are being made to incorporate education as a fundamental right of all children up to 14 years of age in the Indian Constitution so that participation in education by all children becomes obligatory for the state as well as the parents as legal requirement.

— *Community participation* :several strategies such as school mapping and micro-planning are being adopted to ensure participation of people in bringing all children to school and to articulate their demand for improved school services. Community participation is also seen as an essential prerequisite for ensuring long-term sustainability of the initiatives. Participation of NGOs :recognizing the magnitude of the EFA goals and the government resource constraints, the participation of non-governmental organizations and voluntary agencies has been given an important place in the implementation of basic education programmes.

— *Increasing financial support* :considering the need for the development of quality education, the Government stands committed to raise the allocation to education to 6 per cent of GDP as recommended in various national policy documents.

Achievements

Since its inception two decades ago, the NFE programme has consistently grown in size and cover age. In particular, significant expansion of the programme took place during 1990s in terms of the number of NFE centres and the number of children enrolled in them. By 1997, there were 279,000 NFE centres covering about 7 million children in 21 states. Of these, 240,747 are being run by state governments and 37,808 by 544 non-government organizations or voluntary agencies.

Five states –Uttar Pradesh, Bihar, Andhra Pradesh, Madhy Pradesh and Oriss – account for 81 per cent of NFE centres. The spread of the NFE programme is moderate in Rajasthan and Assam. Coverage is very limited in Jammu and Kashmir, and North-Eastern states. The programme started in Arunachal Pradesh during the 1990s. Following re some major points to be noted with regard to progress during 1990s:

— The number of NFE centres increased by 42,000 and enrolment capacity increased by 1 million learners.

— The number of centres exclusively for girls increased by 39,000 resulting in additional enrolment capacity of 975,000 girls.

— The number of NGOs participating in the programme increased by 277 and the number of centres run by them increased by 15,000.

— Annual expenditure on implementation of the scheme increased by about threefold.

As for literacy trends, there has been a substantial reduction in illiteracy, through a multi-pronged approach.

Although with multi-pronged action under formal and non-formal education (including open education/ correspondence courses) and the National Literacy

Mission, considerable progress has been made in reducing the percentage of illiterate population in India, more has yet to be done to completely eradicate illiteracy in order to achieve the concept of EFA.

The National Literacy Mission was established in 1988 with the principal strategy of total literacy campaign (TLC). TLC is delivered through voluntarism by the Zila Saksharta Samitis (ZSS). ZSSs create fusion between district administration on the one hand and volunteer groups, panchayats and social activists on the other. Mass mobilization takes place through multifaceted communication strategy comprising kala jathas, nukkad nataks, wall-writings, padyatras, literacy songs, posters, banners, etc. The teaching-learning process takes 200 hours spread over a period of 6-9 months. Learning materials are developed by using an innovative pedagogy known as improved pace and content of learning (IPCL)

Monitoring and evaluation are done through a periodic system of reporting and through concurrent external evaluation. These are followed by post literacy classes (PLCs) to ensure sustainability of the acquired literacy skills. Some significant facts resulting from the literacy campaigns need to be mentioned. These are:

— community and social mobilization in favour of the idea that learning must become an integral part of life

— increased enrolment of children in schools;

— increased social awareness of the importance of education for parents as well as for their children, especially for girls;

— gender equity and women's empowerment as regards decision-making about themselves, their families and their communities;

— improving the status of women within their own families; and

— improving knowledge about health care and nutrition, thereby enabling mothers to keep their families in better health, to care better for their children's health and hygiene, and to manage their fertility.

About one third of the world's non-literate people reside in India. At the decennial census held in 1991, the most startling fact to emerge was that about 200 million adults were illiterate. India's nation-building efforts began with the severe handicap of extremely low levels of literacy at the time of Independence. The neglect of education during colonial times combined with social distortions had made the quest for learning a difficult and daunting task, especially for those belonging to underprivileged social groups. Saddled with an enormous illiterate population, it was not an easy task to move ahead in the field of literacy and adult education.

After evaluating previous strategies and achievements, the country set up the National Literacy Mission in 1988 and adopted mass campaigning as the mode for spreading literacy. Though the impact, for obvious reasons, may not be uniform across the country. Over all success of the strategy has been well documented. The strategy, coupled with initiatives in the primary education sector, has been able to significantly increase the total literacy rate, in particular in rural areas and among females. Despite the progress, more has yet to be done to completely eradicate illiteracy in India.

The experiences gained so far in the fields of adult and non-formal education must be used to strengthen the current programmes:

Over the years, the non-formal education scheme has given rise to number of innovative experiments by NGOs as well as other implementing agencies. Almost all the major EFA projects have evolved different approaches and institutional arrangements for extending primary education to reach the disadvantaged within the broad framework of non-formal education. Some of these are the Sahaj Siksha programme under Lok Jumbish in Rajasthan and the alternate school programme under DPEP in Madhya Pradesh. This aspect of the scope provided by non-formal education for promoting pluralism and variety in the design and delivery of primary education needs further attention from policy-makers and planners. During 1990s, two features of the non-formal education programmes were stressed. These were importance of making the necessary investments in qualitative improvement of NFE and reiteration that the advantages of NFE lay in its flexibility and adaptability to the needs of disadvantaged children.

Evaluation of NFE programmes has also made sever l useful suggestions for streamlining the organization of NFE schemes, improving infrastructure, qualitative improvement in various inputs, and monitoring with a view to increasing the internal efficiency of the NFE system and enhancing its effectiveness. These factors have to be further strengthened during the years to come.

NFE is a low-cost alternative to formal primary school. However, findings of evaluation of the scheme do not lend support to this assumption. The revised programme of NFE has to aim at delivering "literacy, numeracy and awareness " to those out-of-school children who can not be brought to the formal education system and not cost-saving. This approach places a greater challenge on the government for raising adequate resources for the NFE programme. Despite numerous difficulties encountered and challenges faced, it cannot be denied that NFE has provided access to primary education for millions of children in remote and inaccessible rural areas and urban slums, specially girls and the disadvantaged sections of the society. In that sense, the contribution of NFE in EFA is substantial and significant.

Though the contribution of NFE –about 3.5 per cent of total enrolment at primary stage and reduction of over 1 percent in over all drop-out rate, is quite small when seen in numerical terms, its significance lies in providing an instrumentality for an institutionalized framework for extending primary education to socio-economically disadvantaged children and unreached areas. This should not be lost sight of in assessing the efficiency and effectiveness of the programme.

Partnership with NGOs

A unique feature of the NFE programme is its emphasis on implementation through local and national non-governmental organizations and voluntary agencies. The Government of India has been giving liberal grants to support such activities by NGOs. Participation of voluntary agencies in NFE increased phenomenally during 1990s. While there were 7,310 NFE centres run by voluntary agencies in 1993, their number swelled to 37,808 in 1996 and to 58,788 in 1999. Besides running NFE centres, these NGOs have been implementing 41 experimental and innovative programmes for promoting elementary education. The number of NGOs participating in NFE has been increasing during 1990s.

A problem closely related to universalization of elementary education is that of child labour. According to 1991 census, there were 11.28 million child workers (6.18 million boys and 5.10 million girls) in the age-group 5-14. About 91 per cent of these children are concentrated in the rural areas. Of the 11.28 million working children, 9.08 millions are classified as main workers and another 2.2 million are classified as marginal workers. In addition, nearly 7 million children are enumerated as involved in household duties. Some 6.2 million (88%) of these are girls. Household duties can mean anything from assisting in the family farm or any other family occupation, and taking care of household chores such as cooking, taking care of children, fetching water and fuel, and so on. Thus, if a comprehensive definition of work is taken, the total incidence of child workers is quite substantial and merits serious attention when progress towards EFA is being assessed.

India has all along followed a proactive policy in the matter of tackling the problem of child labour. The Indian Constitution requires the State to protect children against being forced by economic necessity to enter vocations unsuited to their age and strength. However, it should be recognized that the problem of working children and their education can not be treated only as a responsibility of the Labour or Education Department. It is a multi-sector l problem having a direct interface with several other areas of social and economic policy-making.

Keeping these factors in view and in pursuance of the constitutional mandate, the government adopted in 1987, the National Policy on Child Labour, the framework of action with respect to the problem of child labour comprising a legislative action plan, focusing on general development programmes for benefiting children wherever possible, and project-based action plans in areas of high concentration of child labour engaged in wage/quasi-wage employment.

Among the major actions initiated in recent years, one can mention: 85 child labour projects sanctioned in child labour endemic states covering about 130,000 children, the Central Monitoring Committee, under the Chairmanship of Secretary, Ministry of Labour, set up for the overall supervision, monitoring and evaluation of the related projects, and financial assistance to NGOs for taking up welfare projects for working children. Within the education sector, all the major EFA projects have specific components to meet the education needs of the working children. Special attention is paid to the needs of the girl child who is deprived of schooling due to involvement in domestic work and is often not counted as a working child. Special NFE and alternate schooling programmes, including adolescent girl camps, have been designed to meet this requirement.

Indonesia

According to the Law on National Education System, the education system is organized in two different channels, in-school or formal education and out-of-of school or non-formal education. Out-of-school education is based on Government Regulation 73/1991 which states that out-of-school education is aimed at:

- — serving learners by enabling them to develop themselves from their earliest age to improve their standard of living and their self-esteem,
- — helping learners to acquire the knowledge, skills and attitudes needed to develop themselves, to work to

get income and to continue education at the higher level, and

— meeting the educational needs of the community which could not be met by the school.

Out-of-school basic education consists of two packets. The Packet A programme is a non-formal equivalent to the primary education programme and provides both general and vocational education to drop-outs or to those who could not be accommodated in formal schools. The Packet B programme is a non-formal equivalent to lower secondary education programme and provides both general and vocational education to primary school graduates or their equivalency who could not continue education, and to lower secondary school drop-outs. The programme is intended for 13-15 year age-group; however, older students are accepted as well.

Packet B students are not expected to continue schooling after graduation, but if they want to do so they can sit a state equivalency examination and obtain a regular lower secondary school certificate. The learning activity is held three times a week, depending on a consensus reached by the learners, tutor, manager and organizer. Students study with the tutors but must also study autonomously or in small groups outside class time.

The learning content is divided according to lower secondary education curriculum and delivered in the form of modules. Students are evaluated by multiple-choice test on each subject at the end of each semester to determine if they will move on to the next set of modules. The literacy programme is one of the most important pieces of continuing education implemented by the Ministry of Education and Culture since early

1970s. In addition to the nine-year basic education equivalency of Packet A and B programmes, Indonesia continues to run literacy programmes through Packet A, Functional Packet A, and OBAMA which have absorbed a great amount of public budget as investment in human resources. As a result, during the period 1990-1998 the number of illiterate population aged 15-24 years decreased from 1.3 million people to 662,551 people, reduction of 50.4 per cent.

The non-formal education programme (Packets A and B) supporting the nine-year compulsory basic education through the out-of-school education channel. The objective of the literacy programme is to eradicate three kinds of illiteracy: in numeracy and inability to read Latin characters, inability in the Indonesian language, and inability in basic skills.

In order to achieve its objective, the literacy programme is divided into three stages i. e., illiteracy stage, development stage and sustainable stage. The improvement of the literacy programme is carried out through various activities such as research and study, monitoring and evaluation, and through various innovative measures.

In 1995/96 functional literacy was developed in nine provinces with expert assistance provided by World Bank project. The pilot project, after some evaluation and improvement, will be expanded to twenty-seven provinces. Functional literacy is very effective in eradicating illiteracy since it covers the needs and interests of the learners and thereby raises motivation and active participation.

During ten years the programme will cover 10 million people aged 10-44. Each year it will cover 1 million illiterates and 600 thousand semi-literate. In total the illiteracy programme will cover 16.5 million learners, 5 million male and 11.5 million female.

Programmes and Policies

Presently Indonesia is facing a monetary crisis which will affect the enrolment rate in nine-year basic education, transition rate from SD to SLTP, increase the number of illiterates and drop-outs, and decrease motivation of community and family for the achievement of EFA. Therefore, the following strategy and plan of action covering basic learning needs are planned for the next 25 years by the technical working groups of EFA under the supervision of the Coordinating Minister for People's Welfare, such as:

— Increase the transition rate from primary to lower secondary school.

— Provide distance and out-of-school equivalency programmes for children who are not accommodated in primary or lower secondary school.

— Eradicate illiteracy through various innovative and integrated efforts.

— Provide flexible and relevant educational opportunities for drop-outs, the newly literate and graduates of primary, lower and upper secondary education.

— Improve lower and upper secondary school teachers' qualifications.

— Improve the quality of education.

— Increase internal school efficiency.

— Build new schools, new classrooms, and houses for headmasters and teachers

Achivements

Successful campaigns against illiteracy require the involvement of all parties and support of various governmental agencies with similar programme targets. Since 1994/95, implementation of the campaign against illiteracy was developed through the Aksara Manunggal Bhakti Operation or OBAMA. This campaign has the objective of augmenting coordination between the Ministry of Home Affairs, the Ministry of Religious Affairs, the Ministry of Education and Culture, and ABRI (the Armed Forces).

ABRI participates as an operational and a facilitating agent. The Ministries of Home Affairs and Religious Affairs play role in optimizing the utilization of equipment and mobilization of teaching staff under the regional government, as well as the mobilization of prominent local community members. The Ministry of Education and Culture is responsible foratechnical implementation.

In order to motivate the implementers of the literacy campaign programme, a literacy prize competition is organized annually from Kabupaten (district) up to national levels. National level winners are announced during the celebration of the international literacy day. The role of Lembaga Swaday Masy rakat, a non-governmental organization, and social organizations in empowering community members and getting them to join the literacy learning groups is very important.

In fiscal year 1994/95, through the OBAMA project about 1 million participants attended literacy classes. In 1995/96,1 million completed the basic level while another 1 million joined the literacy classes. During 1996/97,1 million joined literacy classes as beginners, 2 million finished the basic literacy level and 1 million were fully literate.

The trends in number of adult illiterates can be described as follows:

— *Illiterate population aged 15-24 years*: The number of illiterates aged 15-24 decreased steadily during the period 1990-98. The majority of young illiterates live in rural areas (bout 18% in 1998 and 87% in 1990). Young females have a higher probability of being illiterate than young males. In fact, in 1990 884,954 female illiterates represented nearly twice the number of male illiterates. Despite significant decrease during the period 1990-98, this ratio remained high in 1998 (i. e., 1.4 times).

— *Illiterate population aged 15 years and over*: In 1990, the number of illiterates aged 15 years and over was 22 million, 20.3 per cent of the total adult population. There were 6,2 million (28.2%) male illiterates and 15,9 million (71.8%) female illiterates. In 1998, the number of illiterate adults dropped to 16.6 million (or 12.1% of the total adult population), comprising 5 million (30.2%) male illiterates and 11.6 million (69.8%) of female illiterates). The only year that saw an increase was 1994 to 1995. The gender disparity also has been slightly reduced as the number of female illiterates for one illiterate male dropped from 2.5 in 1990 to 2.3 in 1998. The proportion of adult illiterates living in rural are has decreased from 86.3

per cent (or 19 million people) in 1990 to 81.6 per cent in 1998 (or 13.6 million people).

Packet A equivalent to primary school: In 1994, the Packet A equivalent to primary school was implemented within the framework of the nine-year compulsory basic education programme. During 1997/98 a National Final Phase Evaluation (PEHAPTANAS) was organized in cooperation with the Examination Centre of Ministry of Education and Culture. Of the 44,803 who is at the examination 40,164 (89.7%) passed. Having succeeded, the participants were given the opportunity to continue studying at an advanced level through formal school or an out-of-school channel. To improve and develop the tutors' knowledge in-service, a tutors' association was established.

The Packet B equivalent to lower secondary school: Since 1998/99, specific skills in agriculture were developed under Packet B learning groups, in addition to the main subjects which are in the form of modules. In order to find out the results of the learning process 1997/98, a national final phase evaluation was organized in cooperation with the Examination Centre of Ministry of Education and Culture. Of the 94,345 who is at the exam 89.6 per cent passed. Some of those who succeeded went on to study at higher level.

The lessons learned from experiences in the past decade will help in developing programmes to make Education for All more meaningful for learners and for society, enhancing learners' development to their full capacity. The following programmes are cases that Indonesia is trying to develop further: Many literate learners do not become literate through attending the learning groups because learning materials do not meet the needs of the learners as regards their survival or improving their quality of life. To overcome this, since 1996 with the assistance of the World Bank and in cooperation with Asian and Pacific Cultural Centre for UNESCO (ACCU)–Japan, Indonesia has started upgrading local staffs to be able to work with learners to develop reading and learning materials more relevant to their learning needs and interests. Furthermore, it is expected that learners will find a true sense of becoming literate for the improvement of their quality of lives.

Education should be relevant to the needs of society, well understood and community-supported if it is to be meaningful. Indonesia has developed an approach known as community-based education through developing a community learning centres. The centres, beginning at the 360 pilot sites, provide community members who are not attending schools with the opportunity to acquire functional and occupational skills.

Such continuing education programmes also upgrade the capacity of community members in rural and poor areas –who are generally lacking in knowledge and information, have limited competencies, lack of achievement motivation, and lack of capacity to change and make progress –in fulfilling basic learning needs as primarily important and urgent needs to be provided. This programme is now encouraged by the Government as a part of the national programme for poverty alleviation.

To prevent school drop-out that may result from the present crisis, Indonesia is launching a programme known as Social Safety Net providing scholarships to students from poorest families to attend basic and secondary schools, and university. Block grants to support running schools in poor areas during the crisis and the budget needed to support out-of-school education programmes are provided, especially for the disadvantaged children who are not attending regular schools. In addition, scholarships are vailable for secondary school drop-outs to attend technical and vocational training courses.

The Community Skill Training Centre has become one of the urgent needs in the Indonesian education system. Such continuing education programmes are initiated and managed by private organizations and business communities who are active in providing training in various skills for community members such as individuals, graduates of various levels and types of education, drop-outs, employees, and housewives. The programmes offered include various types of specialization from sewing, hair-dressing, up to management and banking.

Mexico

The Programme for Educational Development 1995-2000 laid down that basic education for adults would be guided towards the acquisition and the revitalization of knowledge and fundamental abilities. This implies the acquisition of useful knowledge, such as elementary principles of health and hygiene, prevention of illness and household problem; it should encourage diverse forms of skills training and the development of aptitudes needed to carry out a productive activity; and the promotion of values for the full exercise of human rights and participation in a democratic life. Adult and non-formal education consists of special programmes for illiterates and for adults who have not completed their basic education; particular attention is given to initial education activities and ethnic groups are specifically targeted.

There are also open and semi-formal systems foratechnical education and post-lower-secondary schooling. Mexico still has 9 per cent of adult illiterates with a higher rate for women (11%) than for men (7%). Of 62.8 million adult population (aged 15 and over), 32 million have not completed the nine-year compulsory education; 15 million did not complete the secondary school, 11 million have not concluded primary education and 6 million are still illiterate. 26 million adults need in-service training in vocational and technical skills.

The National Training Council for the Life and the Work (CONEYT) was created as an alternative education system with the aim of responding effectively to the needs of in-service training expressed by different socioeconomic sectors. The Council plays the role of an inter-sectoral committee to ensure the educational guidance for youths and adults who were deprived of formal education. In 1981 the different agencies involved in adult education were combined into the National Institute for Adult Education (INEA), which is responsible for the organization and co-ordination of the different programmes of literacy and basic education for adults. The activities of the institute are based on the 1975 National Law for Adult Education. The institute aims to ensure the relevancy of the literacy process for the beneficiaries and to create a productive relationship between learning and their personal and family development.

Programmes and Policies

The literacy and non-formal education programmes aim at reducing illiteracy among the population and to offer alternatives for the completion of primary and secondary education among the adult population. Part of the effort was oriented to vocational training for these adults.

The institute develops its activities by soliciting cooperation within the community and from business enterprises. Young people are engaged to teach illiterates how to read and write in exchange for a symbolic remuneration. Agreements with business enterprises and trade union organizations constitute the framework for the institute's activity. Social mobilization makes it possible to develop solidarity action and to obtain the participation of NGOs and different public organizations interested in employment issues in order to have more resources on adult education and ensure that the education content meet the requirements of the labour market.

The programmes are managed by the federal government, but each state may adapt the programme to its own specific requirements. These literacy actions permitted the provision of basic education and skills training to 2.6 million adults in 1998. A distance education for adults programme was started in 1997 to put into action the constitutional commitment making secondary education compulsory.

Business enterprises and social organizations offer necessary resources to ensure that the workers and other members of the community finish their secondary education. In addition to this type of adult education, there is also training for parents and communities, and for ethnic groups. Initial education is provided through health and social security institutions, and specific activities designed for the different ethnic groups are provided by the Instituto Nacional Indigenista. The several literacy programmes directed to youth and adult populations, developed by the federal government over the past 6 years, included those described below.

— *Alfabetización en español* :aims at helping youths and adults to develop their skills in basic mathematics, reading and writing, thus allowing them to improve their competences in communication throughout their lives. On average, this programme takes eight months to complete; six months are dedicated to the literacy, using the generating word method, and two months to reading and writing with the first Spanish book of primary education. The evaluation of learning in literacy is carried out through two examinations:

  — reading and writing (L1); assess the abilities and knowledge related to word's generation. Success in this examination is a requirement to take the second examination;

  — Spanish 1 (E1):This examination assesses the abilities and knowledge of the first module that corresponds to primary education for adults. The official scale of qualifications ranges from 5 to 10. The minimum qualification for a pass is 6. Passing the exam E1 means that the adult has achieved a level superior to that of primary Grade 2.

— *Alfabetización a groups indigenas* :aims to provide youths and adults from the indigenous population with writing skills in indigenous language and in Spanish. Duration varies, depending on needs and characteristics of each group and the complexity of the language in question. On average, the programme takes 14 to 16 months to complete. The subsidies for this programme re bigger than those granted the programme of literacy in Spanish; this is due to the dispersion of the indigenous population and their high degree of marginalization. This programme has four learning assessments, two more than in literacy in Spanish; this is to ensure that the indigenous population has achieved literacy skills both in their maternal language and in Spanish. Assessment of literacy achievement in indigenous language and in Spanish, and in learning of Spanish as a second language, is conducted using appropriate methodologies of evaluation.

— *Primaria para adultos* :aims to help adults develop their skills and master continuously and autonomously the knowledge corresponding to primary education for adults. On average, it takes 18 months to complete this programme. The diagnosis exam comprises two sessions. To sit for the second session, students must have credits for all the modules of the first session. An adult who passes both sessions can be certified for primary education (intermediate stage) and has the possibilities of sitting for the third session corresponding to the secondary education (advanced stage).

— *Primaria para jóvenes 10-14* :offers the contents of the primary education to children and youths aged 10 to 14 years who did not enrol to the formal education system or who dropped out from schools. On average, it takes 36 months to conclude the programme. The certification process is carried out exclusively through final exams.

— *Secundaria para adultos: aims* at providing the contents of the secondary education to youths and adults who have completed primary education. On average, it takes 24 months to conclude the programme. The adults are entitled to diagnosis exam.

— *Modelo de Educación para la Vida (MEV), Instituto Nacional de Educación de Adultos* :was developed for youths and adults who have not completed a basic education programme; it covers initial literacy (alfabetización) and basic education (1-9). It is currently being piloted in several locations. Evaluation efforts have centred on general statistics information, using mostly state-level databases as sources. Student learning and certification is via multiple choice exams. For information concerning the programme itself, direct observation, field notes, instructor's diaries, surveys and testimonies are the proposed instruments, but have not as of yet been put in place.

— *Educación a Distancia para Adultos (SEA), Secretaria de Educación Publica, Direccion General de Materiales y Métodos* :targets the youth and adult population that has certified 6 years of basic education and that wants to accredit the 7-9 segment. The programme is a distance education model based on printed materials, television programmes and Saturday tutoring sessions. The curriculum and materials are the result of specific effort to cover topics and materials of interest to youth and adults. Student learning is evaluated by multiple choice exams. Programme evaluations include surveys filled out by instructoıs and participants designed to develop a profile of instructors and participants on programme clientele and teachers, and to gather their opinions on the program materials, their design, the information included, the structure of the study sessions, etc. A more detailed and focused evaluation effort is now in place that includes a series of interviews of participants, instructors, and programme co-ordinators.

— *Posprimaria Comunitaria Rural (Consejo Nacional de Fomento Educativo)*:is aimed at the rural population that has completed primary education and offers an open curriculum that develops both academic abilities and locally needed capacities for everyday life. Developed in 1997, the programme was evaluated by an outside agent in 2000. The central interest of the evaluation was to discover the benefits of the project for participants. Research methodology includes visits to 50 per cent of educational centres in two selected pilot states, interviews with students, instructors, and programme co-ordinators. The principal interest in visiting the sites was to understand the different simultaneous processes of the project: how start up is accomplished, how teaching and learning take place, and how student learning is documented. In the beginning the visits and interviews were open until an interview protocol was developed in response to participants' expressed interests and concerns.

Achievements

Different institutions, public and private universities, and the Ministry of Education itself offer open or semi-formal programmes foratechnical and upper-secondary education as well as for higher and graduate education. Most of the population is attracted to open upper-secondary education and graduate programmes for in-service teachers. In addition to activities implemented by the education sector, a new Ministry of Social Development was created in 1992. It offers training activities in accordance with its overall mandate. Since 1996, a computerized system of monitoring and certification (Sistema automatizado de seguimiento y acreditacion –SASA)was set up. This has allowed the Institute (INEA) to have reliable and opportune statistical information, facilitate the administrative work and strengthen the pedagogic and operative aspects such as registration, academic control and follow-up of learners, generation of payrolls, production of reliable statistical reports.

Currently, SASA is generalized throughout the country and complementary modules have been developed to adjust the system to the conditions and necessities of the state institutes or delegations, with the purpose of generating specific information for decisions-making at different levels. Within the educational sector, round 3 per cent of the total budget is allocated to adult education. During 1990s, particular emphasize was made to strengthen the literacy processes of the indigenous groups. The learning methodologies were reviewed, teachers received specialized trainings in indigenous and Spanish language, and pedagogical materials containing regional and cultural peculiarities were conceived. Of the 99,800 natives who benefited of the programme in 1997/98,40 per cent were made literate.

The task of combating illiteracy is made much more difficult as the main target group is older (above 30 years) and/or indigenous using oral tradition. As regards the education of indigenous, the main challenge is to recover the content of the oral tradition that includes the cosmology of these people and whose the means of transmission was mainly "from mother to child ". Thus, a renewed participation of the indigenous women in literacy programmes will ensure in itself a development of their families and communities.

Nigeria

Mass literacy, adult and non-formal education encompass all forms of functional education given to youths and adults outside the formal school system, such as functional literacy, remedial education and vocational education. Adult activities were started informally in Nigeria by itinerant Islamic scholars and traders, the Christian missions and the freed slaves from Freetown, Sierra Leone, at different points since the eleventh century.

The British colonial office recognized these efforts in its Memorandum on Education Policy in British Tropical Africa, published in 1925, which recommended the implementation of an adult education programme in the African continent. In 1930, the colonial government in Nigeria accepted the recommendation and, in 1943, published a document on the subject. Actual implementation started in 1944, although with great limitations.

The training of professional adult educators started in 1965 at the University of Ibadan with the establishment of the African Adult Education Unit. Today, over twenty tertiary institutions (universities, polytechnics and colleges of education) offer degree, diploma or certificate programmes in adult education. Nine states of the Federation (Bauchi, Borno, Kaduna, Katsina, Plateau, Adamawa, Cross River, Rivers and Akw Ibom) have also established institutes where frontline workers in the field of adult education and community service are trained. More than nine states have established centres where adult males and females are taught income-generating skills in addition to basic and post-literacy programmes. In March 1971, the Nigerian National Council for Adult Education (NNCAE) was formed to foster the development of adult education.

The council, which is made up of adult educators from public and private agencies, was largely instrumental to the establishment of an adult education section in the Federal Ministry of Education in 1974. The Council also ensured that the 1975-80 National Development plan had proposals on adult education. It promoted the establishment of Adult Education Divisions in all state Ministries of Education and recommended a ten-year mass literacy campaign for Nigeria, covering the period between 1982-92.

In order to facilitate the achievement of the objectives of the ten-year literacy campaign, it was directed that each state of the federation and the Federal Capital Territory of Abuja should establish an agency for mass education following the models provided by Kano (1980) and Bauchi (1985). Two agencies of the Federal Government –the Directorate of Food, Roads and Rural Infrastructures (DFRRI) and the Directorate for Social Mobilization (MAMSER)–were directed to assist the state agencies in implementing the national campaign. For reasons of funding, logistics and poor planning, very little success was achieved.

Programmes and Policies

The establishment of the National Commission for Mass Literacy, Adult and Non-Formal Education (Decree No.17 of 1990), was partly Nigeria's reply to the international initiative on EFA.

The mandate of the Commission includes, inter alia ; to monitor and coordinate activities relating to the National Mass Literacy campaign in order to ensure the rapid and successful eradication of illiteracy in Nigeria; to monitor and coordinate the implementation of all activities for the eradication of illiteracy in Africa and ensure the collection and dissemination of information on literacy implementation in the continent; to conduct research in various fields such as curriculum development, learning and teaching methodologies, appropriate education technologies, motivation of learners and instructors, and needs assessments; and to commission special research programmes and pilot projects in mass literacy adult and non-formal education in Nigeria.

According to the National Policy on Education, the goals of mass literacy, adult and non-formal education shall be: to provide functional literacy and continuing education for adults and youths who have never had the advantage of formal education or who did not complete their primary education, including nomads, migrant families, the disabled and other categories or groups; to provide functional and remedial education for those young people who did not complete secondary education; to provide education for categories of completers of the formal education system in order to improve their basic knowledge and skills; to provide in-service, on-the-job, vocational and professional training for different categories of workers and professionals in order to improve their skills; to give the adult citizens of the country the necessary aesthetic, cultural and civic education for public enlightenment.

To attain these goals, the Federal Government established a National Commission for Mass Literacy, Adult and Non-Formal Education. As a complement to the effort of the Federal Government, each state established a mass literacy agency as part of the overall national effort to eradicate the illiteracy. The Commission monitors and evaluates the mass literacy programme and facilitates communication between the commission and state agencies.

Achievements

Since its inception, Nigeria has featured prominently, winning Honourable Mentions seven times, but the real literacy prize came in 1989 when the Adult Education Department of the University of Ibadan was warded the Literacy Prize of the International Reading Association. The Department has since recognized that only community-based literacy programmes can survive in rural areas where tradition is strong and the outsider is suspect. It was the realization of this fact that led to the Department's Community Development Literacy and Health Project which began in 1989 as a special contribution to literacy promotions. This project metamorphosed into the University Village Association (UNIVA) a non-govern-mental organization seeking to build a bridge between the university and the community, and between theory and practice in Adult Education, contributing to policy formulation and literacy promotion, offering seed money to participants in the literacy classes to enable them to initiate small-scale enterprises.

At present, UNIVA is one of the best known non-governmental organizations involved in rural development in Nigeria. UNIVA began as a literacy project, promoting the co-operation of the university academic community and the village communities for development purposes; it has been transformed into a movement and an expression of community ownership of programmes.

This development has provided a vitality and invigoration that explains the sustainability of the project, now embracing health issues, democracy and good governance, economic ventures and functional literacy for adults and youths in especially difficult circumstances, for women and for minority groups. Not unexpectedly, UNIVA became the first and at the moment the only non-governmental organization in Nigeria to be commended for its intervention in literacy promotion in Nigeria by UNESCO when in 1997, it received Recognition by the Jury for the International Literacy Prizes for the "excellent work "that it has done. Again, in 1999, UNIVA received the Honourable Mention for the Malcolm Adiseshiah International Literacy Prize.

UNIVA, founded in 1989 with the support of the International Foundation for Education and Self-Help (IFESH), shares the burden of development with government following its conviction that illiteracy limits the capacity and full potential of the individual in the performance of most skills and in having access to useful information that can facilitate the making of important choices.

In ten years, UNIVA has produced over 5,000 literacy learners, over 1,000 of whom have undertaken post-literacy work. All the learners have had a heavy dose of functional literacy. UNIVA has extended its work to urban areas among mechanics, market women and street children. It has also produced materials and strategies that have proved capable of attracting learners to the classroom.

With community participation, multi-purpose centres have been built in villages and are used for income generating promotion and health talks. UNIVA has succeeded in mobilizing learners by adopting a dignified recruitment and retention strategy. With its meager resources, UNIVA has succeeded in assisting both rural and urban people of Oyo and Osun States in overcoming their illiteracy, health and economic problems. The income-generating programme has helped to improve the economic status of the participating men and women.

Enrolment progression in adult and non-formal education: In 1991, total of 546,256 males and females were enrolled in adult education programmes. It is encouraging to note that more women are increasingly showing interest in non-formal and adult education programmes; the proportion of enrolled women increased from 43.2 per cent in 1991 to 49.2 per cent in 1996.

Increased enrolment in mass literacy programmes: A total of 3,985,987 male (85%) and 3,266,357 female (45%) were enrolled. The same pattern of more male than female enrolments is observed. The steady rise in enrolment in the early 1990s peaked in 1993 with a total enrolment of 1,076,110. Also significant is the percentage of female participation in the programme.

The most serious weakness in the Nigerian mass literacy, adult and non-formal education between 1994 and 1996 was the acute shortage of data on the subject. What existed were pieces of information occasionally put together by various implementing agencies to satisfy required needs as they arose. Unfortunately this cursory information remains unreliable and unverifiable. Thus, the setting-up of a good statistical information system is one of the important challenges, since data constituted the basis for policy formulation and planning.

The establishment of the National Commission for Mass Literacy Adult and Non-Formal Education in 1990 marked a turning point in the development of adult education in Nigeria. The Commission not only monitored and co-ordinated adult education programmes and activities but also served as clearing house for collection and dissemination of information on adult educational programmes. Thus by 1999 the task of procuring basic data on various aspects of adult education had been made easier, the focus of adult education programmes was clearer and the performance of adult education projects was easier to quantify.

With regard to national population it would appear that the adult component of the population of Nigeria which stood at 88.9 million in 1991 was close to 110 million by the year 2000. The implications of this growth in population for adult education programmes were immense, necessitating remarkable increases in the level of funding, further enrichment and review of the curriculum, considerable expansion and improvement of existing physical facilities, and the establishment of a more network for monitoring and inspection.

As more youths drop out from school and as the national economy continues to depend on acquisition of skills in non-formal setting as opposed to mere possession of certificates, enrolments in adult education programmes will drastically shoot up creating enormous pressure on the existing facilities. One of the gre test challenges of adult education programmes in Nigeria in the foreseeable future is the ability of the programmes to attract the adult youths to rural environment through the establishment of cottage industries.

From the present picture, the literacy rates of females in rural settings appears relatively low, at least far below the national figure. Enrolment progression in adult and non-formal education in Nigeria between 1991 and 1996 would appear fairly impressive, rising from 546,256 in 1991 to 926,132 in 1995 and then to 1.14 million in 1996, representing a gross increase of 597,481. From the analysis by gender, relatively more women have been participating in adult educational programmes.

Using the average growth rate of 2.6 per cent experienced since 1991, enrolment progression was projected up to the year 2004. From that projection, enrolment in adult education programmes would reach 5 million by 2004. Clearly the challenge for adult education programme in the next five years would be more of ensuring qualitative development rather than a mere emphasis on quantitative growth.

The overall performance of learners in adult education programmes in Nigeria is fairly disturbing. For example, out of the 1.14 million learners who enrolled in the various programmes in 1996, only 487,662 were awarded certificates. It is interesting to have figures broken down to indicate how many enrolled but did not complete the programme, how many completed the programme but did not sit the test and how many is at the test but were not warded certificates. From all vailable studies, the facilities in adult education centres are poor.

Most of the centres lack standard basic facilities. The checklist survey done by SAPA showed that a lot of improvement still need to be carried out in the are of physical facilities for adult education centres. The situation is so bad that in some cases, classrooms, classroom furniture and toilets were not vailable.

It is very difficult to ascertain the level of funding adult education programmes in Nigeria. This because government is at local, state and federal levels have not fully committed themselves to formal development of adult education. There is the tendency to rely on donor agencies, mostly in the United Nation system and non-governmental organizations, for funding adult education programmes. When this is the case, the donor agencies insist on the commitment of counterpart funding before releasing their grants. In situations where counterpart funding is not forthcoming, the targeted adult education programmes are wholly or partly abandoned. It would appear that the poor quality of instruction at adult education centres is largely responsible for the low performance of students. The problem of instructors is two fold: the problem of qualification and the problem of remuneration.

Understandably emphasis is placed more on experience and acquired skills than on paper qualification in the determination of who qualifies to teach in adult education centres. Similarly a situation where instructors in adult education centres, whether part-time or full-time, are paid as low as 500 nairas month is deplorable. This probably accounts for frequent reports of absenteeism of instructors and their lack of commitment in the performances of their duties.

Based on the above observations, the following recommendations were formulated:

— The National Commission for Mass Literacy, Adult and Non-Formal Education should be further strengthened financially and structurally to ensure greater impact at local and state levels. Greater emphasis should be made in the areas of coordination, reinforcement of state and supervision and inspection.

— Regular research on the utilization of the learners who have passed through adult education programmes, especially as regards their impact on the national economy and employment, should be encouraged and conducted. Such studies, properly conceived, should attract the assistance of donor agencies.

— To identify the pressure of national population on adult education programmes, it is essential to develop a master plan for mass literacy, adult and non-formal education in Nigeria up to 2010. Such a master plan will not only guide governments at local, state and national levels but will also assist international organizations in identifying their interests in the are of assistance.

— Deliberate efforts should be made to attract the Nigerian population, particularly those in the rural areas, to adult education programmes. This can be done with the development of incentives to young adults wishing to settle in rural areas. Such incentives should not only include ready access to adult education programmes in rural areas but also the granting of small scale loans and facilities to young adults who come together in co-operative societies and who intend to establish home-based industries and small business enterprises.

— To increase the level of interest of rural women in mass literacy and adult education, centres for both basic literacy and post-literacy programmes should be established in nearby market places where most of the women converge.

— Mass mobilization of women's societies, particularly in the rural areas, should be organized to sensitize their members to the need for literacy in their everyday life. To ensure equity in the distribution and location of adult education centres; there is greater need for their efficient planning and monitoring.

— To ensure qualitative development of adult education programmes: a clear emphasis should be made in improving the existing facilities, ensuring a steady supply of trained and experienced staff, and increasing the level of funding.

— The present curriculum of adult and non-formal education programmes should be reviewed to include areas that have direct relevance to the young adults. Apart from basic literacy, emphasis should be placed on direct and indirect employment, and self-employment programmes.

— Research should be conducted on the performance of learners to determine the reasons why some learners enrolled but did not complete, why some completed the programme but did not sit the test and why some who sat the test were not warded certificates. There is an urgent need to improve the physical facilities in adult education centres in Nigeria. Such facilities should emphasize availability of classrooms, classroom furniture, basic teaching and learning equipments, and toilets.

— It is absolutely necessary for governments at local, state and federal levels to clearly identify funds for adult education and demonstrate greater commitment to its regular financing, just as regular funding is clearly determined for formal education. As one of the strategies for improving the quality of instruction in adult education centres, urgent attention should be given to the problem of poor remuneration of instructors. While a statutory salary structure may not be the answer, it is essential that adequate incentives be given to instructors in adult education centres as a motivational strategy as well as strategy for improving the quality of their teaching.

Pakistan

Literacy programme in Pakistan could not be institutionalized. The Prime Minister's Literacy Commission at the federal level and the Education Departments and non-governemental organizations at the provincial and local levels re running literacy programmes. Baluchistan is the only province with a separate directorate of non-formal education, under the Social Welfare Department, running number of literacy programmes at provincial level.

Adult literacy has not been given the requisite and desired attention and focus in Pakistan, neither in terms of programmes and projects nor in terms of budgetary resources and finances. Data vailable indicate that provinces as such do not allocate any budget for literacy. However, the federal government has earmarked some financing for the promotion of literacy and mass education but it is meagre and insufficient in view of needs of the country. Total current expenditure for literacy is only Rs.179 million over period of nine years. Sindh is the only province to have allocated some funding i. e. Rs.23.88 million for adult literacy. The development expenditure during the post-Jomtien decade was Rs.651.7 million. The major chunk, i. e. Rs.590 million, was made under federal budget. The provinces of Sindh and Balochistan allocated Rs.41 million and Rs.13 million respectively.

Despite the prevailing high illiteracy rate, only a few projects and programmes for eradication of illiteracy were launched during 1990s and they do not measure up to the challenge of making literate some 42 million of adult illiterates. The major literacy projects and programmes launched and implemented during the 1990s include: The Prime Minister's Project of Eradication of Illiteracy, The Prime Minister's project of "Establishment of 10,000 Non-formal Basic Education Schools ", The Quranic Literacy Project 1992-94, The Crash Literacy Programme and the Literacy Programmes run by non-governmental organizations.

Programmes and Policies

The Pakistan National Education Policy planned to increase the literacy rate to 70 per cent by the year 2002.

The target for 1995 had been set at 50 per cent. The provincial governments, NGOs and local institutions are actively involved both in planning and implementation. Allocation for adult literacy programmes will be substantially enhanced at the federal and provincial levels.

The main programmes, agreed strategy and plan of action to achieve the literacy goals and targets as reflected by the National Education Policy, the Social Action Program (1998-2003) and the Nineth Five-Year Plan (1998-2003) are as follows:

— The literacy programmes shall be implemented through provincial governments, NGOs and local organizations.

— Literacy programmes will be integrated with skill-based community development programme.

— The post-literacy phase will be made an integral part of all literacy programmes. Greater attention will be focused on the deprived segments of society in rural areas and urban slums, with special emphasis on the female population.

— The strategy of achieving 100 per cent literacy in selected areas will be carefully employed to produce the emulative effect.

— The potential of electronic and print media will be fully utilized for motivating the public at large, for supporting literacy effort and for delivering literacy programmes. Appropriate legislation will be enacted by the provincial governments, patterned on the Literacy Act 1987, to provide incentives for acquiring literacy.

Achievements

The results of the literacy policies can be assessed with regard to particular projects implemented during the 1990s.

Eradication of illiteracy from selected areas of Pakistan: This project was launched by Prime Minister's Literacy Commission with a total cost of Rs.72.83 million from 1992-94. The target was to make literate 174,460 adults (both male and female). Salient features of the project were as follows:

— Opening of 3,460 face-to-face literacy centres and 200 television literacy centres in five selected districts: Islamabad, Hafizabad, Karachi East, Quetta and Tehkal Bata, and Peshawar.

— Implementation through non-governmental organizations and community groups with strong motivational drive.

— *Area-specific approach*

  Under this project 138,025 (79%) adult illiterates were made literate against the target of 174,460. Out of these 120,082 (87%)were females and 17,943 (13%)males.

— *Quranic literacy project 1992-94:* This project was initiated in 1992 with a cost of Rs.4.06 million to make females literate through their knowledge and reading skills of the Holy Quran. The project wanted to find out whether females who are able to read/ recite the Holy Quran can be made literate in Urdu with greater case and in a relatively short period of time. A special primer was introduced for this purpose. The project was trialed in five union councils in four districts surrounding Islamabad; 494 face-to-face centres were established at places provided by the community. Teachers were paid honoraria of Rs.500. In all, four cycles of six months each were completed. Some 10,867 girls and women aged 10 and over were made literate through this project. The limitation of this programme re as given below:

— Timetable arrangement sometimes kept some of the literacy teachers busy throughout the day as all the learners were not able to attend the centres at the same time.

— There was no incentive, in any form, for the learners. As a result, drop-out could not be prevented.

— The rural community is very much busy in marriage ceremonies, harvesting work, festival ceremonies, death functions, etc., and hence, total number of days devoted to learning during the six-month cycle was much reduced in many cases.

— In one district, parents hesitated to let their girls learn to write although they let them learn to read.

– *Establishment of 10,000 non-formal basic education schools*: The Prime Minister's Literacy Commission in 1995 formulated a project titled "Establishment of 10,000 Non-formal Basic Education Schools " at a total cost of Rs.1,263 million and to be implemented within a five-years period. The project, based on the idea of home school to be run through non-government organisations and community-based organizations, was launched in April 1996. In the first financial year 1,052 non-formal basic education schools were established with a total enrolment of 31,560 students. In the next financial year, another 6,065 non-formal basic education schools were opened throughout the country. The financial allocation for 1996-97 was Rs. 241.3 million, later reduced to Rs100 million and as result, the project suffered a major setback. The teachers did not receive their salaries in time and the students did not receive books and learning materials.

The Education Policy (1998-2010) recommended expanding the programme by opening 75,000 non-formal basic education community schools during the next three years. The Prime Minister, while announcing the National Agenda, emphasized universal literacy for children and set up a committee to prepare an action plan. The Action Plan also recommended the expansion of non-formal basic education community schools programme. On 11 July 1998, ECNEC approved the expansion of the programme from 7,000 to 82,000 non-formal basic education community schools with a total budget of Rs.11.2 billion and the programme is included in the SAP II. However, expansion will only take place after an evaluation of the existing schools by the third party.

The salient features of the project are:

— Basic education schools are established in those areas (villages or hamlets) where government primary schools are non-existent, or where separate schools for girls are not vailable, or where girls' participation rate at primary level is low, or where female illiteracy is pronounced, or where the drop-out rate is higher.

- Basic education schools offer learning opportunities to out-of-school children aged 5-9 and mis-outs/drop-outs aged 6 to 14.
- An educated person, preferably a trained PTC, to be contracted for the task with a fixed emolument of Rs.1,000 per month. In case a trained PTC teacher is not vailable at local or village level, secondary school graduates are considered. In the backward areas, the educational qualification is also relaxed.
- Teaching aids such as black boards, charts, mats, etc. for students are provided by the government.
- Learning materials in the form of books, note books, pencils, slates, etc. are supplied to learners free of cost.
- Curriculum for the formal primary school system is used for all children of age 5-9. Whereas, a condensed non-formal primary level basic education course has been developed for drop-outs and out-of school youth of age 10-14 and above.
- New entrants, or children aged 5-9, take three to four years to complete the primary level course, depending upon their learning pace and efficiency of the teacher.
- Preference has been given to the establishment of schools for girls.
- Final examinations are conducted by examination teams headed by authorized representatives from District Education Offices. Graduates of non-formal basic education schools are eligible for admission in the sixth class in formal schools.

— Schools function in locals provided free of charge by the community. These may include public places, Mosques, community centres, buildings made vailable by philanthropists, or at teachers' residences. For drop-outs and mis-outs aged 10-14, existing school buildings can be used in the evening, where possible.

— *Crash Literacy Programme*: Ministry of Education planned a Crash Literacy Programme in May 1998. The purpose of the programme was to increase the participation rate by making maximum use of the vailable resources such as school buildings and teachers during summer vacations and evening hours. This programme aimed to promote literacy and basic education. To make the programme cost effective, existing schools buildings with all the infrastructure of shelter and supplies were used as literacy centres. The qualified teachers vailable during summer vacations were engaged for the programme and paid nominal honorarium for this extra duty after a short training programme.

The students had no school uniform obligation and were provided with free textbooks and learning materials. The centres were located close to the majority of the beneficiaries/out-of-school children. The programme began in the Federal Capital District of Islamabad and in the province of Punjab as a pilot project. The salient features of the programme re as follows:

— Focus has been given to rural girls/female illiterates and to providing a second chance to out-of-school children within the aged 6-14.

— Some 87 literacy centres have been opened in the Federal Capital District of Islamabad and 222 schools in the Province of Punjab.

— For each centre or school, the services of a teacher were provided. Teachers were paid Rs.

— 1,500 per month as salary/honoraria in the Federal Capital District of Islamabad and Rs. 1,000 in Punjab.

— The syllabus prepared by Allama Iqbal Open University was selected for the course. Teaching and learning materials were selected from the literacy materials developed through national workshops as well as books and primers used in formal schools. Literacy teachers were given brief orientation/training course.

— A literacy campaign was also launched to create awareness amongst the target groups.

— In Punjab, students were paid Rs.20 per attendance as an incentive.

— Learning material was provided free of cost.

— The unit cost of the programme was around Rs.1,900 per student.

The output of the programme can be assessed in two parts:

— *Federal Areas Programme*: Under Federal Areas Crash Literacy Programme about 87 literacy centres were opened in three phases, with a total enrolment of around 1,500. Assessment or evaluation tests conducted by the Ministry indicated that 82 per cent passed. Moreover, the literacy programme created awareness amongst the masses and local communities who were motivated to play an effective role in the eradication of illiteracy. Total cost of the project was only Rs.6.4 million.

— *Punjab Literacy Pilot Project*: The Punjab project was successful in terms of enrolment. The target of 5,550 students was fixed and the Department was able to meet 60% of the target. In a few girls' schools,, enrolment exceeded the maximum number of 25 students per class and the girls in excess of the maximum limit attended the centre without any financial incentive. This showed encouraging prospects, as was the number of parents willing to send their children to formal schools after the Pilot project.

Encouraged by the results of this project, the Government of the Punjab is undertaking the Phase II of the Programme, with a tenfold expansion. The enrolment target is 50,000 students for which 1,668 centres catering to 30 students each would be opened. The honoraria of teachers was raised to Rs.1,500 with added financial incentives related with the results of the final examination. The monitoring system has also been strengthened and the course contents have been revised. The Government of the Punjab intends to continue with this project on even larger scale after Phase II, expanding the project in terms of enrolment and in terms of community support. Total cost of the project was Rs.10.5 million.

— *Literacy programmes run by NGOS:* The programmes launched by non-governmental organizations in basic education and literacy at the provincial and local levels re in addition to the above. Some of the programmes run by well-established non-governmental organizations are reported to be very effective and productive. Non-governmental organizations have been actively involved in the promotion of literacy and adult education since 1990. In 1992, the non-governmental organizations were involved in the project namely "Eradication of Illiteracy from the Selected Areas of Pakistan ". Since then, the non-governmental organizations have been playing an increasingly important role in literacy and non-formal education. The Adult Basic Education Society (ABES) and BUNYAD in Punjab, SHOAA Balochistan and the Khyber Welfare Association in North-West Frontier Province were the non-governmental organizations involved in the Pilot Literary Projects.

The estimated adult literacy rate is 45 per cent. The high illiteracy rate among rural women is one of the major constraints in achieving EFA goals and the overall development of the country. A critical review of literacy programmes, plans and strategies adopted in Pakistan indicates a number of weaknesses and shortcomings which need to be addressed on a priority basis so as to achieve the literacy targets set at national and international levels. Among the most salient weaknesses, one should mention:

Adult literacy has not been given needed priority in EFA programmes. Only a few projects on adult literacy could be launched during the post-Jomtien period; their coverage was limited and restricted to not more than 10 per cent of the target group. Resources earmarked for adult literacy programmes were amounted to barely 1 per cent of the education budget and funds could not be provided on time.

Coordination among the principal actors in the field of adult literacy remained weak. Monitoring and evaluation mechanism at grassroots level could not be strengthened, which adversely affected the internal efficiency and effectiveness of the literacy programmes and projects. As a result, the country with 45 per cent literacy rate fell short of the 70 per cent literacy targets set at World Conference on Education for All (Jomtien,1990) and in the National Education Policy 1992. The female literacy rate was under 33 per cent in 1998. In view of the high population growth rate, the inadequacy of resources, the slow pace of educational development and other such factors, the targets set in adult literacy were too probably ambitious to be achieved in such a limited time.

4

Status of Basic Education for Adults

The 1990 World Conference on Education for All, held in Jomtien, Thailand, but the concept of "education for all" on the world's agenda and led to widespread commitment to the goal of "meeting basic learning needs" of all persons, whether they be children, youth or adults. Significant progress has been made toward this goal during the 1990s. Most of this progress, however, has taken the form of increased enrolments of children in formal schooling. While universal access to schooling is crucial, extending basic education to children is only part of the picture. Masses of illiterate and poorly educated adults are still inadequately prepared to take their places in the emerging global society as parents, workers, and citizens.

Renewed attention to basic education for adults is thus necessary to stem the divisive and destructive forces of polarization and marginalization. Marginalization occurs when people are systematically excluded from meaningful participation in economic, social, political, cultural and other forms of human activity in their communities and thus are denied the opportunity to fulfil themselves as human beings. When a critical mass of individuals and entire groups become marginalized, society itself becomes polarized. While the marginalization of even a single person is a human tragedy, the polarization of entire societies is both tragic and dangerous.

Yet, we appear to be moving toward world in which wealth of all kinds of economic assets, social capital, political influence, knowhow and information is being concentrated in the hands of a privileged few. Simultaneously, a growing proportion of humanity is effectively excluded from access to such riches and from meaningful participation in the modern world.The forces of exclusion are at work within and between industrialized and developing nations alike. Evidence of the resulting marginalization can be seen in the latest data on rates of literacy, which correlate strongly with other symptoms of marginalization.

Countries that have already achieved a comfortable level of economic development are in a better position to take full advantage of the forces shaping the world of the 21st century, while other countries are not. The industrialized countries provide schooling to virtually all children and have a rather small pool of illiterate adults, while the developing countries as a group still fall short of providing universal primary schooling and have a very large pool of illiterate and semiliterate adults. In other words, the "haves" are in position to get richer, while the "havenots" are likely to get poorer. Even in situations where the living conditions of some developing countries are improving, the "haves" seem to be advancing even more rapidly, thus increasing the gap between them and the "havenots".

The least developed countries are home to an ever-increasing proportion of the world's illiterate population. However, the positive news IS that they, together with the other developing countries, are also home to a growing number of the world's literate adults. Within industrialised countries'-

Large numbers of people find themselves marginalized even within nations that rank among the "haves". The Organization for Economic Co-operation and Development (OECD) estimates that there are 20 million jobless and 38 million poor in Western Europe. In 1995 there were also an estimated 9 million illiterate adults in Europe, of whom two-thirds are women. Two recent surveys, the Young Adult

Literacy Survey (YALS) and the National Adult Literacy Survey (NALS), used direct measurement of skills to determine the extent of illiteracy in the United States of America. They found that less than five percent of Americans aged 21 to 25 could not read or write at all, but almost a quarter had problems reading texts that required more than simple decoding. Similar studies in Canada came to similar conclusions.

An "explosion" of organized adult learning activities is now under way in industrialized countries, but that the benefits of these activities are unevenly distributed. Adult education services tend to cater disproportionately to those who are already educated, already employed and younger rather than older. They also cater disproportionately to men, who are more likely than women to have their studies paid for by employers. A "dual learning society" is emerging in the countries studied. For better and for worse, participation in adult education is a "cumulative social practice". "Just as the participants accumulate advantages, the adults who did not have access to prolonged initial education will tend to participate much less and will have to overcome important sociocultural barriers."

A similar warning was issued by the report Lifelong Learning for All, prepared for the January 1996 meeting of the OECD education ministers. It noted that the emerging "learning economy" is now accommodating a growing share of the workforce in industrialized countries but added that "the divisions between those who are included and those who are excluded are sharp and could deepen".

Marginalization is also a growing problem within countries that rank among the "have-nets". In many developing nations economic and other resources are concentrated in the hands of a relatively small ruling elite. Efforts to increase the social, economic and personal welfare of the citizens of such nations sometimes have the unfortunate side effect of exacerbating existing differences. For example, schooling often benefits persons living in urban areas more than those in rural areas, in countries across the development spectrum. The gender gap in educational opportunity feeds other forms of polarization, including disparities in the status of men and women. The marginalization of girls and women is a problem that exists to some extent in virtually all nations, but it is especially profound in the developing world and notably in rural areas, as seen in adult literacy rates.

Social Transformatiion: Effects on Basic Education

Recent years have brought a breakdown in the single-party political systems in many nations, most notably those of the former Soviet Union, and a substantial increase in the number of countries with democratic forms of government. Such changes have meant that millions of persons now have the opportunity for the first time to participate in politics and exercise influence over their lives and destinies. According to Freedom House, a nonprofit and non-partisan organization in New York established in 1941 to promote democracy around the world, the number of countries that now meets its criteria to be considered "free" or "partly Free" has increased over the past decade.

Democracy, though, makes demands on its citizens. To work well, it requires an electorate that is informed about issues and that has the motivation, skills and confidence to participate in decisionmaking. In order to have an informed electorate, basic education must be extended to children and adults alike. In the absence of a well-educated citizenry, power tends to be appropriated by a ruling elite, and the problems of marginalization and disenfranchisement persist.

A variety of forces, including the growth of a global market economy and the discrediting of centralized governance, has led many states to diminish their traditional role in redistributing wealth and providing social benefits and services in respect to education, health, transportation, communications and so forth. This trend can be dated to the oil crisis of 1973 when industrialized countries of the West discovered that the welfare systems financed by the post-World War II economic boom could no longer be sustained. These systems also faced increased political pressure from leaders such as Ronald Reagan, Margaret Thatcher and other proponents of laissezfaire capitalism and a reduced role for government. The fall of the Berlin Wall and the collapse of communism contributed further to this erosion of the state's responsibilities.

The new governments m central and eastern Europe lack both the political mandate and the financial means to fulfil the role of the former socialist state as guardian of the social safety net. The retreat of the state from its redistributive role is often presented as an inevitable development, as a law of nature as meluctable as the weather. What is often overlooked, however, is that this change has involved political choices and, one must add, political failures. Political leaders have, quite simply, often failed to meet their social obligations. Such failures have contributed to the economic and social marginalization of large numbers of people. Education as a polarizing force.

One unfortunate fact of life is that education, seen by many as a means of promoting equality, functions too often as a source of inequality. Those who have a good basic education are in position to benefit from further education. Employers train the trainable, building on the skills employees bring to the marketplace from school or nonformal programmes. To those who have, more shall be given. As "lifelong learning" becomes more established, the gap is likely to widen between those who have a sufficient basic education to benefit from further learning and those who do not. In Sweden, for example, participation in employer-sponsored education programmes ranged from 69 per cent for some professional groups to 15 per cent for some unskilled blue collar groups.

John Ryan, a UNESCO literacy specialist, sees much of the problem as lodged in thinking that views education as an 'investment'requiring a maximum return. By such logic, employers prefer to invest only in workers who need relatively little further training to upgrade their skills. Such thinking flows from the fact that most employment-oriented training is funded by private enterprises.

New information technologies represent a structural break with the past. Patterns of implementation are uneven, and those having experience with the first generation of a new technology are better prepared to take advantage of subsequent breakthroughs. Thus the macro forces discussed earlier can combine with formal schooling to form a vicious circle that widens the gap between those who are poorly prepared to face life and those who are armed with the knowledge and skills to defend themselves and take advantage of opportunities.

The economic, social and political costs inherent in these trends toward the marginalization of large numbers of people and the polarization of society are enormous. Excluding large numbers of people from participating in the changing world economy runs the risk of creating enclaves of poverty, despair and violence that cannot be eliminated by last-minute government action or humanitarian aid. This is true in industrialized as well as developing countries.

In a recent controversial article entitled *The Capitalist Threat,* George Soros, a financier whose credentials as a successful capitalist are beyond dispute, warned that the current widespread faith in unrestricted free markets portends serious danger to the concept of an open society. "By taking the conditions of supply and demand as given and declaring government intervention the ultimate evil," he wrote, "laissezfaire ideology has effectively banished income or wealth redistribution [...I Wealth does accumulate in the hands of its owners,, and if there is no mechanism for redistribution, the inequities can become intolerable." Soros criticized social Darwinism as a basis for organizing human affairs. He wrote that "there is something wrong with making the survival of the fittest a guiding principle of civilized society" because "cooperation is as much a part of the system as competition".

Basic education empowers individuals because it opens up avenues of communication that would otherwise be closed, expands personal choice and control over one's environment, and is necessary for the acquisition of many other skills. It gives people access to information through both print and electronic media, equips them to cope better with work and family responsibilities, and changes the image they have of themselves. It strengthens their self-confidence to participate in community affairs and influence political issues.

Basic education is the key with which individuals can unlock the full range of their talents and realize their creative potentials. It gives disadvantaged people the tools they need to move from exclusion to full participation in their society. Basic education also empowers entire nations because educated citizens and workers have the skills to make democratic institutions function effectively, to meet the demands for a more sophisticated workforce, to work for a cleaner environment, and to meet their obligations as parents and citizens.

One irony of the "knowledge explosion" is that it renders basic skills more essential than ever. In order to move into the mainstream of the society, marginalised people do not need special forms of education: they need solid training in literacy and numeracy skills, basic scientific concepts and, above all, they need the capacity to continue acquiring new knowledge and skills.

Access to basic education is a fundamental human right. It is also the essential precondition for the effective exercise of other human and legal rights. The Universal Declaration of Human Rights, adopted by the United Nations in 1948, asserted that "everyone has a right to education," and this position has be embraced and further elaborated in several subsequent normative instruments adopted by the world community. In 1990, during International Literacy Year, the World Conference on Education for All reaffirmed the right to education when it adopted the World Declaration of Education for All.

Article I of the Declaration affirms specifically, "Every person child, youth and adult shall be able to benefit from educational opportunities designed to meet their basic learning needs." Article 3 added that "basic education should be provided to all children, youth and adults" and declared that "for basic education to be equitable, all children, youth and adults must be given the opportunity to achieve and maintain an acceptable level of learning".

In a formal sense adult basic education can be thought of as all forms of organized education and training, including literacy instruction, that meet the basic learning needs of adults. Adults are usually defined for statistical purposes as persons aged 15 years or older. Technically, the term "literacy" refers to reading and writing skills, but many adult literacy programmes today are organized around broader aims and content than just literacy and numeracy. The term is sometimes used also with reference to various other kinds of basic knowledge and skills such as "scientific literacy", "computer literacy" and "political literacy."

The phrase "meeting basic learning needs" means different things in different circumstances. The knowledge and skills that a farmer needs to be an active participant in a rural community differ from those appropriate to a government worker in an urban capital. Moreover, learning needs change over time and basic education should, too.

Forty years ago, Thailand set out to provide two years of basic education to all children. Over the years the sights were raised, two years at a time, to twelve years at present, and the country is now working on legislation regarding adult education. In countries that have recently moved toward democratic forms of government, the concept of "political literacy" becomes an important part of basic education..

For some time to come, however, efforts will continue to be necessary to promote literacy in its original sense in order to move towards basic education for all, especially in nations where illiteracy among adults is widespread. The emergence of "knowledge-rich societies" and "learning economies" organized around the creation and manipulation of knowledge, information and ideas will place new demands on adult basic education. Furthermore, the aging of the population in many countries calls for diverse and flexible approaches to adult learning because senior citizens now have more time available to them and a variety of interests and activities.

Educators around the world are increasingly recognizing the importance of moving beyond a narrow concept of adult basic education. The World Declaration of Education for All states: "To serve the basic learning needs of all requires more than a recommitment to basic education as it now exists. What is needed is an expanded vision that surpasses present resource levels, institutional structures, curricula, and conventional delivery systems while building on the best in current practices."

Many studies have reported and even measured the positive correlation between parents'educational levels and the attendance and performance of their children in school. In general terms, children whose parents have at least a basic education tend to do better in school than children whose parents have had little or no education.

The test scores of pupils improve as the level of parental education rises. In this case, it appears that the mother's level of education has more effect on pupils'performance than does the father's

A survey in Nigeria found that among several "home background" variables, the fathers'educational qualification was the most predictive of pupils'performance in school, accounting for I 9 per cent of the variance in pupils'scores. In Lebanon, another survey focusing on fourth grade pups found that "the lower the parents'education levels are, the lower their children's achievement levels will be".

An earlier study in Sri Lanka also looked into home background factors that affect children's learning. "In general, the educated parents always try to provide their children with some education.... Most educated parents support learning at home of their children by providing additional reading material such as newspapers, magazines, etc. The study analysed the variance of pupils'test scores according to whether the parents regularly, sometimes or never "encourage encouragement for children's learning is not necessarily related to the educational level of the parents.

A survey in Mauritius found "Children from families with low socioeconomic status received less support at home than those from better-off families. On the other hand, parents with low educational qualification were more likely to help their children in school than parents who had high sometimes or never "encourage learning", or "support learning" or "supervise work". It found that "The encouragement given by parents for the education of their children is seen to be contributing to the learning achievement at school." However, parental encouragement for children's learning is not necessarily related to the educational level of the parents.

Among the several factors that influence children's learning, the education of parents is clearly very important. In fact, some basic education programmes cater particularly to young adults of child-bearing age and deaf with family matters and child care in the lesson materials. Efforts of this kind can enhance the inter-generational effects of basic education to the advantage of children and adults and how well they do is the level of education of their parents. Such findings are well known m industrialized countries, but it has also been shown that in developing countries, the children of parents who have at least a basic education do better in school. This is especially true of girls with educated mothers.

Such findings make intuitive sense. Parents, along with other members of the family and community, are the child's first teachers. Educated parents understand the value of education and communicate this to their children. They are more diligent in assuring attendance and organizing household affairs so that their children have the time to study and attend school. Thus it follows that investing in the basic education of adults especially those adults with the most influence on the next generation will not only produce better educated adults but pay off in better educated children as well.

Awareness of the importance of investing in the education of parents is growing. In all societies, the best predictor of the learning achievement of children is the education and literacy level of their parents. Investments in adult education and literacy are, thus, investments in the education of entire families. Schools alone cannot do the job of bringing about universal basic education. Although formal schooling has had great success in most industrialized nations, they still have large pockets of illiterate and poorly educated people.

Changing World, Changing Educational Concepts

The world is changing so fast that even if everyone completed compulsory schooling, people would still need more education, However, a period of initial schooling that equips all children with the basic knowledge, skills, values and attitudes they need to function in their communities and to continue learning throughout life will continue to be necessary, though not sufficient by itself. A sound strategy to provide basic education for all requires a combined effort to improve and expand basic learning opportunities m school and out-of school for children, youth and adults. Any strategy that relies on the primary school alone, in the absence of complementary measures, will fail to meet many basic learning needs and is likely to be inefficient. Furthermore, a sound strategy must take into account that the effectiveness of basic education is strongly affected by forces beyond the control of schools.

Adult basic education encompasses a wide variety of activities, some well-established, while others are struggling to survive. Adult education is a long-standing tradition in the Nordic countries, especially in Sweden, where large numbers of adults have participated in "study circles" since the 1970's. Debate is now underway about the equity of such programmes, with critics arguing that the courses intended for under-educated Swedes tend to be of short duration and do little to address fundamental educational disparities.

The best-known adult education movement in the developing world is the "conscientization" approach inspired by the Brazilian educator, Paulo Freire. Through his book *Pedagogy of the Oppressed* and other writings, Freire argued that if adults are given a chance to engage in active learning, they will become aware of the nature and causes of social oppression and gain the tools to participate in actions toward social change. This concept of popular education expanded throughout Latin America during the late 1960s and remains a potent force. The projects it generated are small and localized, however, so its overall quantitative impact is said to be rather limited.

There have been several examples of successful, national mass literacy campaigns over the years. In some countries, such as Cuba, Nicaragua, Viet Nam and

Somalia, their "one-off" campaigns were undertaken soon after revolutionary movements acceded to power and enjoyed widespread popular support. In Ecuador, however, the government showed that it was possible to mobilize young people to teach literacy on a volunteer basis in a nonrevolutionary setting.

Other adult education programmes are as different as the settings where they are carried out, and many combine literacy instruction with other social objectives, For example, the Roman Catholic Archdiocese of San Salvador uses its radio station to provide basic education to children, youth and adults, while China has organized 200,000 "parent schools" attached to formal schools to educate citizens about health, nutrition, child development and other matters. Indonesia has a large-scale programme to educate mothers on the care of children between birth and age three, while Nepal operates a programme that uses textbooks in the form of comics to approximate the first three years of formal primary school for adults who have little or no schooling. The principal organizers of many such programmes in developing countries are non-governmental organizations (NGOs), most of which operate on a small scale.

Eradication Adult Illiteracy

The ranks of the literate adult population in the world are growing, though the patterns in the industrialized and the developing countries are sharply different. The number of literate men and women in the world is increasing: and this growth is expected to continue for the foreseeable future. At the same time, the number of illiterate adults has remained at about 885 million since

1980 and, if present trends continue, will remain largely unchanged through 2010. This constant core group of illiterates, almost two-thirds of them women, persists over time despite efforts that are increasing both the number and proportion of the literate population in the world.

All regions have made progress in narrowing the gender gap in adult literacy rates, but significant regional disparities remain. Improvements in literacy rates have been more pronounced among younger age-groups. Data on the distribution of the adult population by level of educational attainment also show substantial regional disparities. The countries in some regions, notably sub-Saharan Africa and South Asia, have large proportions of adults who either have no formal schooling or have an incomplete primary education. These adults constitute the primary target group for adult basic education.

There is a strong possibility that these statistics understate the extent of adult illiteracy because many countries use years of schooling as a proxy indicator for literacy. This does not take into account that adults with poor literacy skills that are seldom used often relapse into illiteracy. Yet, on the eve of the 21st century, most children in most countries have at least a few years of schooling, so the number of "true" illiterates who have had no instruction is probably declining. On the other hand, the number of individuals with poor literacy skills is probably growing, and as the requirements of the workplace increase, these people will find themselves increasingly marginalized.

Participants in the mid-decade meeting of the EFA Forum in Amman Jordan, in June 1996, examined the question of whether the world was moving closer to the goal of universal basic education agreed at the Jomtien Conference in 1990. "In the six years since the adoption of the World Declaration on Education for All," they wrote in the final communique, "there has been significant progress in basic education, not in all countries nor as much as had been hoped, but progress that is nonetheless real."

The major gains came in expanded primary schooling. The communique states: "Primary school enrolment has increased, an estimated 50 million more children were enrolled in 1995 than in 1990. The number of out-of-school children, which had grown inexorably for decades, is also beginning to decline." It went on to say that attendance gains were accompanied by "a growing emphasis on the quality of education". While celebrating such gains, the Forum warned against oversimplifying the problem and focusing only on primary school enrolment. "The expanded vision of basic education espoused in Jomtien has often been reduced to a simple emphasis upon putting more children into school: an essential step, but only one of many measures needed to achieve EFA," says the Amman Affirmation.

Participants were concerned that there was little information available on adult basic education, with the exception of reports from a few countries such as India, Namibia and South Africa, that have launched major adult literacy programmes in recent years. The final report of the Amman meeting noted, "Many participants felt that the strong emphasis given so far to expanding schooling has obscured other dimensions of EFA and particularly its agenda for meeting basic learning needs of people of all ages needs that evolve over time and tend to become more sophisticated." Despite the commitments made at the Jomtien Conference, the funding of adult basic education is precarious in nearly all countries.

Empowering Adult education Programmes

Adult education programmes can be powerful instruments for promoting economic, social and political objectives. But the purpose of education must not be restricted to "fitting" human beings into the production process or into various social institutions. Education has two other important functions.

First, education equips individuals to develop and express the full richness of their particular personalities and talents in the various roles they play in society. In other words, education empowers people.

A. Lind's evaluation of the national literacy programme in Namibia described the empowering nature of that project. Learners reported feelings of "coming out of darkness" and increased self-confidence and self-reliance in dealing with banks, post offices and hospitals. At the community level, Lind reported, the greater sense of self-esteem that came from literacy led learners to become more active participants in meetings and organizations. They typically expressed reactions such as, "I am now somebody and have something to say. Before I used to remain quiet and felt very stupid".

Another function of education, in John Ryan's words, "is to instill in individuals the need and duty to make all aspects of life fit for human beings." Until now, adult education in the industrialized and developing countries has tended to respond to the needs of the economy, but has focused hardly at all on more social and cultural purposes.

The World Declaration on Education for All took note of these broader purposes of education: after reaffirming the right of individuals to have their basic learning needs met, it went on to state, "The satisfaction of those needs empowers individuals in any society and confers upon them a responsibility to promote the education of others, to further the cause of social justice, ensuring that commonly accepted humanistic values and human rights are upheld, and to work for international peace and solidarity in an interdependent world." .

One innovative approach to literacy instruction that goes in this direction is REFLECT (Regenerated Freirean Literacy Through Empowering Community Techniques), started in 1993 by ACTIONAID, a British non-governmental organization, and piloted in some 100 villages in Uganda, El Salvador and Bangladesh. This approach, which builds on the theories of Brazilian educator Paolo Freire, has each literacy group develop its own learning materials using maps, calendars and diagrams that represent local situations and help the group to analyze and organize their knowledge. Using locally designed visual cards, graphics are transferred to paper, and each participant creates a book with phrases he or she has written. Evaluations of the pilot experiences suggest that this approach not only teaches people to read and write and enhances their self-esteem, but it also prompts learners to take actions at the community level to improve living conditions. Learners have taken greater control of household decisions and resources, showed greater awareness of health issues and improved the school attendance of their children.

Adult basic education can play a significant role in achieving such objectives. Through the acquisition of basic knowledge and skills, individuals can gain the tools and self-confidence to become productive workers, citizens and family members, and fulfil themselves as human beings. The importance of education as an engine of economic development means that, for the first time, countries lacking in natural resources or large amounts of capital are no longer doomed to poverty. The coming of a world where ideas have greater value than petroleum is a welcome development.

The most challenging fact in the foregoing analysis is that there are still nearly one billion illiterate adults in the world, and the number will probably stay at this level into the next century unless large-scale and determined efforts are made to reduce it through a combination of universal primary schooling and adult literacy activities.

The world community and each individual country thus face a choice. They can stand by while the forces of marginalization and exclusion exact their toll on individuals and whole societies, create the seeds of conflict and anti-democratic forces, threatening the very stability of world order. Or the nations of the world can make the necessary investments to address marginalization and polarization m their many faces. Of course adult basic education is no panacea. Concerted efforts are necessary on economic, social, political and other fronts. But ensuring that all adults acquire a basic education, whether through primary schooling when they are children or through basic education programmes for adults, is an important starting point, and without gains on this front little else will be accomplished.

5

Promotion of Education and Literacy in Rural Areas

Vision goals are appropriate for any organisation that wants to strengthen its own accomplishments or position in the economy or society. An electronics company, for example, will set its vision in terms of gaining significant market share in its products, or earning a reputation as the manufacturer of the highest quality electronic appliances worldwide. A ministry of education will.set a vision of building a school system that allows every child to acquire a good-quality primary education; a teachers college will aim to ensure that every teacher is well trained. For the electronics company, the ministry of education, and the teachers college, these visions are suitable and may well be feasible.

Even though non-formal education is often a unit of the ministry of education and therefore expected to function like a formal school system, in fact it is very different. A formal school system is intended to meet the common needs of all children to acquire accredited basic skills and to channel them through the system, with increasingly diverse—but very limited—options as they mature. Non-formal education, in contrast, picks up the pieces and looks for those whom formal education has missed.

The clients, or beneficiaries, of non-formal education are not longer in the system. In fact, it is their "outsideness" or disadvantage that brings them into touch with non-formal education programs. Thus, to set a goal of meeting the needs of all disadvantaged men, women, and children is not likely to be feasible through a single, monolithic program and therefore not very "strategic." Because non-formal education is aimed at different groups with different needs and requiring different approaches, strategic goals in non-formal education programs are better conceived in terms of problems that must be solved.

Let us look more specifically at goals in the area of literacy. Educational officials generally includes literacy among the programs of the expanded non-formal education department. They were midway into a nationwide campaign in basic literacy. Once the campaign had been completed, how should they define a new goal in the area of literacy? They considered two alternatives. One alternative was in terms of a vision: for example, making every youth and adult self-sufficient in literacy. This would entail a post-literacy campaign to follow up the basic literacy campaign, providing out-of-school youth and adults with training that would consolidate their literacy skills. In order to be rolled out efficiently, such a campaign would have to rely on a fairly standardised curriculum. Yet learners who have been given basic skills, come to a post-literacy course with different levels of competence, different needs, and different interests. A standardised course would be difficult to teach in these circumstances.

An alternative goal was in terms of a problem: breaking the barrier between out-of-school youth and opportunities for their participation in productive work, community involvement, and family care. This would entail a variety of integrated literacy and practical skills training programs, each aimed at a specific group of adolescents or adults who had opportunities for immediate application of their new literacy skills. Instead, the goal of a literacy program should be set in terms of problem solving. For example: The goal of the organisation is to improve the management of crop pests by teaching farmers to read information on integrated pest management. Or, the goal is to reduce childhood illness by teaching mothers to read simple healthcare manuals; or, to improve civic responsibility by teaching community members to read locally published newsletters.

In formal education, policy-makers, teachers and administrators can more or less dictate what students must learn and even how they must learn, because they hold the keys to certification and advancement through the system. Educators in non-formal programs do not have these incentives to offer. They can only attract people who want to learn something in order to improve their lives and or to gain access to opportunities otherwise out of reach. In other words, people who choose to participate in non-formal education programs are usually those who have taken responsibility for their own learning and achievement. An effective non-formal education program recognises this important quality of its learners and keeps the learner in control of his or her learning. So one principle guiding non-formal education is that the learner must be allowed to take charge of his or her own learning. A corollary is that communities of learners must be encouraged to take responsibility for opportunities for their members to learn. A good non-formal education program begins with activities that ensure that the community is in charge and that providers of education are following their lead.

A second principle is that non-formal education providers must be responsive to learners' needs and interests. One size does not fit all. This means that non-formal education providers must help create curricula and materials that respond to the specific needs of specific groups of learners. The provider must work with the group to clearly identify the problem to be solved and the resources needed to solve it.

A third principle is that, more often than not, those resources will entail more than just training. For example, women in a community who want some economic freedom may need credit, equipment, and supplies as well as skills training. The non-formal education provider may not furnish more than training, but it may need to help the women find the complements to the training that will make it useful.

These three principles—learners taking responsibility for their own learning, providers responding to learners' needs, and the need for resources that complement training—argue against nationwide campaigns or other programs that put the government in the driver's seat and deliver a "one size fits all" package throughout the country. Unlike formal schools, with their uniform, nationwide curriculum—at least through the junior secondary level, each non-formal education program is targeted to a small, difficult-to-reach group of learners, who learn only when they take responsibility for doing so.

Most developing governments, had been putting a much larger portion of its national budget into primary education over the last decade. With its limited monetary resources and pressure for financing of higher and secondary education as well as primary education, the ministry had little left for non-formal education. Many non-formal education programs had already been well established by non-government organisations and other government agencies.

Unlike the formal system, where the government's goal is to envision and build a system that accommodates all children and most youth, the government in non-formal education can help those who have missed out on the formal school system—to incorporate training and education into the solution of their problems. Instead of helping teachers and administrators authorise students to move from one level of the system to the next, the non-formal education department can help non-formal education providers to authenticate courses that have practical, immediate application in learners' lives.

Instead of a uniform formal curriculum, the non-formal education department can foster myriad curricula. Instead of maintaining professional support systems such as teacher training colleges, and administrative and infrastructure support systems such as payroll and construction, the non-formal education department must encourage disparate groups of learners to find their own support. These tasks are not easy, and they may explain why governments and funding agencies are much more willing to build large school formal systems than to support the non-formal education sector.

Promotion Nonformal Education: Pilot projects in Asian Countries

In many Asian countries the major task for is to expand provision and services of basic education to those who have not yet had access and are under-served by the existing regular literacy and basic education programs. One major segment of the unreached population in respect of literacy and basic education, especially in the South Asian countries, are girls and women. UNESCO' s Asia-Pacific Program of Education for All (APPEAL) has, since 1992, supported two programs.

The first is a series of pilot projects for promotion of primary education and literacy with a special focus on girls and women in rural and disadvantaged communities in China, India, Nepal and Viet Nam.

The second is a series of pilot projects for promotion of literacy among youths and adults in Bhutan, China, Lao PDR and Nepal. The aim of these pilot projects is to develop innovative and effective strategies and approaches for promoting literacy and basic education in support of larger national programs. Financial assistance has been provided to the two projects under the Japanese Funds-in-Trust for Promotion of Literacy in Asia and the Pacific.

The main support and assistance provided under these projects were in the form of training for teachers/ facilitators; development of curricular and teaching-learning materials: involvement of local communities for genuine ownership of programs, and encouraging central/local governments' interest in alternative forms of literacy and basic education for all.

Although the main objective of these pilot projects is promotion of literacy and basic education for the disadvantaged and under-served in rural and difficult areas, their emphasis on content, materials and strategies adopted in each participant country have been tailored differently to respond to specific needs and circumstances.

Specifically, projects in six participating countries have undertaken their work with the following emphasis:

— In Bhutan, the project was initiated at two learning centres in a rural district to provide non-formal education for youth and adults, which has been expanded in co-operation with UNICEF, to all over the country.

— China has carried out two projects: one for promoting literacy and quality of life of ethnic minorities living in rural areas; and the other for promoting girls' education in formal primary schools, as well as introducing non-formal education strategies for extremely disadvantaged groups. Both projects have created explicit links between additional income generation skills and education/literacy.

— In India, the project has assisted in enhancing regular primary education, especially for girls in disadvantaged areas, through developing handbooks and training of trainers with a focus on raising awareness of gender equity issues. This is seen as a foundation activity for other initiatives.

— In Nepal, one project has emphasised non-formal primary education through various Lead Centres and Learning Centres to increase the educational opportunities of out-of-school girls in disadvantaged areas, while the other project has targeted farmers in poor economic condition to promote literacy and improve living conditions.

— Viet nam has focused on improving education for girls in ethnic minority groups through non-formal primary education programs and school based income-generation activities. In Lao PDR, the project has provided literacy programs for selected rural villages with particular reference to income generation and quality of life programs through community learning centres.

These pilot projects have contributed quite effectively to the promotion of literacy and primary education at the project sites. They have identified certain important aspects concerning the provision of basic education for rural disadvantaged areas. One of the lessons learnt and reinforced from the projects in all the participating countries is that curriculum contents and materials need to be closely linked to the local situation and needs. In most of the participating countries, efforts have been made to develop learning skills which incorporate quality of life features such as health, nutrition, respect for one' s own culture and entrepreneurship.

An evaluation meeting on the pilot projects for promotion of primary education and literacy was held in Manila from 1 to 3 May, 1997, in cooperation with SEAMEO INNOTECH. Prior to this meeting, each country carried out an evaluation exercise with guidelines provided by APPEAL. The purpose of this evaluation was to assess the impact of these pilot projects, to identify successes, problems and bottlenecks, and to describe effective modalities of the projects. Evaluation reports were prepared and presented at the Manila meeting in order to share experiences.

The following is an overview of the two pilot projects namely, promotion of primary education for girls and disadvantaged groups; and, promotion of literacy for youth and adults.

Promotion of primary education for girls and disadvantaged groups

China

The project in China targeted poor girls from ethnic minority populations living in Gansu province. These girls faced social, economic and cultural barriers to The focus of the project was to change traditional beliefs by creating a positive school environment, introducing new experiences and extending schools to become community development centres. The project mobilised parent and community involvement, improved school quality through mobile teacher training teams, established pre-school classes, and linked functional literacy classes to vocational skills training. The enrolment and participation of girls improved through changed attitudes of the community to education and literacy. Similar projects have been implemented in the provinces of Ningxia, Qinghai and Guizhou under the support of the Chinese government.

India

The project targeted Haryana, a province like many others in India, where the status of girls and women was very low due to social and cultural attitudes. It is characterised by a low sex ratio for females and poor enrolment to of girls in schooling. The focus of the project was to sensitise and orient educational administrators and teachers to gender issues and women's empowerment.

The project provided are source base from which training materials could be developed. Thesewere used in conjunction with both orientation programs for educators and awareness campaigns at the village level. Materials were also developed for teacher training programs. A state-wide capacity for training of gender awareness has been an outcome of the project. Furthermore, teacher training institutes now provide gender equity issues as part of their programs.

Nepal

The project sites were based in 3 districts of Nepal, namely Kathmandu, Diraha and Kailali. All were characterised by having low enrolments and highdrop-out rates for girls. All communities were poor with an agricultural economy. The focus of the project was to provide a non- formal structure for out- of -schoolgirls. Through sensitisation of parents, the project also encouraged neo-literates to enrol in the formal school system.

A "Lead Centre" was established to function as are source centre for learning. The program used an approach which linked literacy materials with the daily activities of the girls. An attempt to make the community aware of the benefits of education for girls was made by in volving parents in education and through advocacy campaigns. In addition, skills training in sewing was also provided. The major outcome of this project was that 80% of girls graduated from the non- formal programs subsequently enrolled in the formal system.

Viet Nam

The project targeted girls from poor ethnic minority groups living in remote mountainous regions. The project has been carried out in selected ethnic minority areas in four provinces namely, Ninhbinh, Lamdong, Lao Cai and Ha Bat. Prior to the project, there was low participation and high drop-out level among girls in these areas. The focus of the project was to meet the learning needs of the girls in the context of their lives. Furthermore, activities were held to make parents-aware of the value of girls' education. School activities were linked to income generation schemes such as the school garden (raising pigs and fish and planting vegetables). The Vietnamese acronym for this was "VAC". Schools became more "girl friendly" by providing toilets and making the environment more attractive.

The project resulted in largely improved participation and drop-out rates. The income generation projects were successful and acted as a catalyst for changing attitudes of people to the value of girls' education. It is planned to expand the project to other districts and to other provinces under the support of UNICEF.

Promotion of Literacy among youth and adult

Bhutan

The project targets poor farmers who have never had the opportunity to receive education. The project started by establishing five pilot centres in the districts of Wangdi, Pemagatshel, Thimpu and Trashi Yangtse. With Thimphu support from UNESCO and UNICEF, it is being expanded to a total of 15 districts. The focus of the project was to provide functional and skills-based literacy training and to promote the national tongue. Non-formal centres were established, based on existing schools and in private homes, and were staffed by trained instructors. Special curriculum materials for life skills, reading and mathematics were developed and utilised.

There were improved literacy skills as a result of the project and local people had a more positive attitude to literacy training. In addition, elder people were motivated to learn in order to help their grandchildren and to further participate in their religion.

China

The target for this project was a poor rural community living in mountainous areas of Guizhou province. Although this community lived in a fertile area, per capita incomes were still very low and poverty was a major constraint. The focus of the project was to eradicate illiteracy and to provide farmers with practical techniques for self improvement through additional income generation activities. Women were a special target of this project. A close link between literacy programs and practical technology classes was established to reinforce the benefits of being literate. Motivational campaigns were carried out in order to recognise and reward literate families.

The project resulted in significant improvements in both literacy rates and private incomes. Through the practical technology classes, farmers were able to significantly boost their incomes. In the case of female farmers, this resulted in women having a greater social and economic role and status.

Lao PDR

This project was based in Salavan province, a southern area still recovering from the effects of war. In addition to chronic poverty, villagers were also afflicted by malaria and cholera. The focus of the project was on providing literacy and skills development through the provision of non-formal programs. A revolving small loan scheme for initiation of income generation activities was also linked to participation in literacy programs. The project supported textbook development in literacy, health and basic skills development such as chicken farming and weaving. Local people were trained as non-formal facilitators and an awareness program to highlight the importance of literacy was mounted. As a result of the project, improved participation in educational activities has occurred.

Nepal

This project targeted poor agricultural villagers living in Sarlahi, a southern plain area prevalent to diseases. Low literacy rates were prevalent throughout the area. The focus of the project was to eradicate illiteracy and provide non-formal activities for out-of- school students and those who had dropped out. Women' s literacy courses were a particular target.

A village readiness program was the initial activity of the project. The project also developed new materials and curricula approaches for the literacy classes which were subsequently introduced. The major outcome of the project was seen in the increased number of non-formal graduates who wanted to continue their education with further courses. The project also acted as a catalyst for villagers in wanting improved infrastructure and income generation training.

Exchange of Experience

As a regional project, UNESCO PROAP has organized the following activities to facilitate sharing the experience among participating countries, in order to develop the scope and strategies of project planning and implementation:

— Joint planning meeting for: primary education project (Thailand, 1991); and, literacy project (Thailand, 1991)

— Project review meeting for: primary education project (Nepal, 1993, and China, 1995); and, literacy project (China, 1995)

— Evaluation meeting (Manila, 1997)

— Presentation of the projects at Asia Literacy Regional Forum (Manila, 1997) Study visits by projects teams from China, Lao PDR, Nepal and Vietnam (1993-1996).

Country Experiences: Major Impact and Success

The following two tables present a summary of country reports on the evaluation of the pilot project. While Table 1 shows an overview of the project on girls and disadvantaged students, Table 2 presents an overview of the literacy for youths and adults project. These tables do not attempt to describe the individual projects in a comprehensive manner; rather, they present the major issues and problems.

Summary of Country Reports

	China	India	Nepal	Viet Nam
Targets	3 poverty stricken counties with minority populations	Girls in a province where all gender indicators were low	Literacy and income generation for girls	Ethnic minority girls living in mountainous regions
Context	ER-9 1%, Repetition = 17% Dropout = 5°/ Girls have barriers for schooling by social, cultural, economic and educational factors Low literacy rates	Low sex ratio of females Low status of females State commitment to education Improving infrastructure	Girls ER = 37% Girls dropout rate = 70°/. at Grade 1	High drop-out (45-100'/.) Low participation rates
Focus	Change traditional beliefs on education Create favourable environment Explore new experiences Rural schools as community development centres	To sensitise and orient administrators, teachers, educators to gender issues	Provide non formal structure for out-of-school girls Encourage neo-literates to enrol in formal schooling Sensitise local community for girls education Skill training for girls	Meet the learning needs of girls in ethnic minorities Give basic skills,knowledge Show significance for girls Prepare curriculum and materials Have activities for parents

Methods	Mobilise parents and community Training of educators Advocacy materials Combine literacy skills with vocational skills Pte-school classes	Build a resource base Collaboration from state Training materials made Orientation programs for educators Awareness campaigns at village level	Parents aware of education Involve parents in education Develop/exhibit materials Street drama, videos,	Monitoring committees Teacher training courses Develop curricula, materials. local skills, knowledge Train the community Social awareness and VAC tarining
Outcome	Enrolment up by 11Yr Retention up by 3 % Repetition/dropout by g/2% Pilot schools are models	Generate state level capa cities in gender training Teacher training in gender issues	Material for keywordmethod NFE for out-of-school girls Skill training (sewing) Higher no. of irks in FE	Improved participation and drop out rates Relevant content in school VAC profit for school use
Notes	Project relevant to local needs Collaborative partnerships	Societal and economic factors lead to gender gender discrimination	Parent programs well received but poverty means immediate I benefits needed	Responsibility contracts between schools, parents and communitiessigned
Problems	Lack of funds - sustainability Personnel stability Closer link to poverty alleviation	Lack of female teachers	Traditional beliefs Lack of motivation Timing of NFE classes Economic constraints	Quality of education Poverty and remoteness Lack of local teachers Teacher ability to make aids

Table 2. Youth and Adults

	Bhutan	China	Lao PDR	Nepal
Targets	People who have not received education	Poor rural community in agricultural area	Province devastated by war Ethnic minorities	District with low literxy rate 5 villages, 10,000 population
Context	Poor farmers who have missed out on education	Mountainous area with good soil	Problems of poverty, malaria and cholera	Languages other than Nepali, diseace prevallant
Focus	Functional and skill-based literacy training Promotion of national language Provide post-literacy & continuing education	Eradicate illiteracy Farmers to obtain practical techniques for self improvement (income)	Promote literacy Training of NFE staff Provide skills development	Eradicate illiteracy, provide for Outof-xhool & dropouts Women's literacy emrsec Post-literacy courses Micro-planning carried out New methods of teaching
Methods	Curriculum development of life skills, reading, maths Local officials involved School-based NFE centres Separate NFE section NFE pedagogy for teacher training courses Better Selection of NFE instructors	Literacy classes & practical technology classes together Publicity campaigns Local materials Community involvement "Literate Family.' awards Visiting teacher model for women Population schools	Textbooks developed for literacy & skills development Raising community awareness by giving skill development Local people trained as facilitators	Needs analysis & new muerials, curriculum developed Village readiness program Train facilitators, supervisor Implement literacy classes

Outcome	Improved literacy skills Attitudes to social/ economic environment changed Elder people want to be involved	Local curriculum & texts implemented for farmer cultural & technical schools Training for community awareness Improved literacy rates	Improved participuion in school Community awareness of educational benefits Increased income from additional skills	Health & sanitation better School enrolments better Literacy graduates want to enrol in post-literacy courses Community interested in income generation schemes
Notes	Time available to learners does not match availability of facilities	Women now have a greater socio-economic role & status A 300°/, increase in pc income over project life	A revolving fund to stimulate income generation linked to skills training is successful	A common question by community was "After basic literacy, what next
Problems	Time constraints due to farming cycle Lack of props facilities Monitoring of Progress Caring for young children prevents attendance Slow progress leads to lower motivation CHINA	Lack of funds Insufficient training Lack of full-time practical skills instructors	Literacy content must reflect daily life Changing social- economic model, introduced by Govt. causes cultural problems Slow progress leads to lower motivation	Poor involvement by NGOs & community leaders Lack of micro planning Irregular supervision Inappropriate methods used Village committee inetfectivc Poor fxilities (lighting) Ethnic ianguage problem

A thematic analysis of experience under the country projects is presented below:

Project on Promotion of Primary Education for Girls and Disadvantaged Groups

Targets: All projects were based in rural areas with poor populations. Ethnic minority populations were a specific target in China and Viet Nam. Girls were the prime target in the India and Nepal projects although other projects also included girls.

Context: All projects had in common school aged populations with low participation rates, high repetition, high drop-out rates and low levels of adult literacy in the local community. China and India reported specific cultural barriers to girls' participation in education.

Focus: The project in China had as a focus the changing of traditional beliefs concerning education. It explored new experiences to create a more favourable environment where schools also acted as community development centres. The project in India had as a focus, attitudinal change among educators to gender issues and the empowerment of women. Providing non-formal structures and sensitising the local community to girls' education was the focus of the project in Nepal while the Vietnamese project aimed to meet the learning needs of girls in ethnic minorities by making schools more "girl friendly".

Methods: All projects had in common the mechanism of mobilising parents and community for greater involvement in education. The Indian and Nepalese projects used awareness campaigns as the major technique while China and Viet Nam used a specific link between education and skills development for income generation as their prime methodology.

Outcomes: The projects in China, Nepal and Viet Nam all reported improved participation, repetition and drop-out rates. Improved capacities for gender training, both in the community and in teacher training programs, was an outcome of the project in India. The projects in Viet Nam and China were also successful in facilitating communities to improve their incomes.

Problems: Economic constraints and community poverty were experienced by all projects. The Chinese report indicated a need for a closer and more explicit link between education and poverty alleviation. The Nepal project was constrained by traditional beliefs about education and a lack of motivation on the part of students. Viet Nam recognised a need for more local (local culture and language) teachers and India a need for more female teachers.

Project on Promotion of Literacy for Youths and Adults

Targets: All projects targeted poor rural populations who had missed out on education and where literacy rates were very low.

Context: All projects were situated in remote provinces where farming was the main source of income. The Lao PDR project was also characterised by a population who were still recovering, both socially and economically, from the ravages of war and were still facing problems of malaria and cholera. The Nepalese target group were also confronted with diseases such as encephalitis.

Focus: The focus of all prqjects was on the provision of literacy classes. These classes were directly linked with skills development programs in Bhutan, China and Lao PDR. Nepal also included a focus on new methods of teaching.

Methods: The Bhutan project used NFE centres, based in existing schools and developed curriculum in life skills as well as in reading and writing. China linked literacy and practical technology classes and used public recognition of literate families as a motivating mechanism. The Lao PDR project raised community awareness by providing literacy programs and skills development in basic agricultural areas. Nepal implemented a "village readiness" program together with newly developed curricula materials and a pedagogy designed for adult learners.

Outcomes: Improved literacy rates were reported in all projects with the Nepal project also experiencing an increased demand for subsequent formal school enrolments. Attitudinal changes were seen in the projects of Bhutan, China and Lao PDR with education being viewed more positively. China and Lao PDR reported significant increases in per capita income as a result of skills development activities.

Problems: Bhutan experienced a problem of available facilities and personnel not matching the time constraints of farmers caused by the cycle of agricultural activities. Insufficient training, particularly the lack of full-time technical skills training, was the major problem reported in the China project. Lao PDR reported a problem of the content of literacy programs not matching the daily lives of people. In addition, the rapid social and economic changes occurring in Lao PDR caused confusion among remote villagers. The Nepal project was hindered by inappropriate teaching methods and a lack of involvement by key community leaders. Poor infrastructure together with difficulties related to the ethnic minority population were also a problem.

Synthesis of Country Reports

The summary of country reports indicated that a number of dimensions were common to all projects. These are summarised below. The various projects are at different points on these dimensions. However, it is important to note that all dimensions relate to the likely sustainability of the project once external funding ceases.

1. *Decentralisation of project components*

All project reports refer to decentralisation as an important aspect of project implementation. Generally, decentralisation occurs through the involvement of local committees who have varying degrees of influence and authority. However, it is not apparent that local community involvement occurred during the planning stages of projects. As a result, the following questions might be posed:

— Is decentralisation really happening or does it only involve a token involvement of the local communities in the planning and implementation of the project?

— Decentralisation should occur for training, curriculum, management, control, and ultimately, authority and responsibility.

— Do local communities have the skills and knowledge to carry out these functions?

— If they do not, should the project have as an initial objective, the transfer of these skills to local communities?

— One comment presented was: "We can' t make villagers think that this is their program ." Is this because they were not involved in the planning as well as the implementation of the program?

2. *The link between the world of work and educational/ literacy programs*

All projects recognise the importance of literacy being a means to an end, with the end being initially an improvement in quality of life through increased income. However, projects varied in the directness of the link between literacy and increased income. In some cases, for example China, identification of new income generating schemes was relatively straightforward since they needed only to be linked to food production. However, in other cases, such as Lao PDR and Nepal, alternative and viable income generation schemes were not easily identifiable. The following questions might then be presented:

— How can the projects link education and literacy programs to the local context of work?

— Can the projects examine and quantify social and economic rates of return for education and literacy programs?

— Can the projects clarify and demonstrate the benefits of education, even though there are foregone earnings (labour) while learners are at school? For example, a farmer may have a lower income while attending a literacy program but does his/her income increase significantly after completion of the program? Are there role models to demonstrate such benefits' ?

3.Demonstration of how education and literacy will result in a better life

Awareness campaigns and other publicity techniques promote the view that education will result in a better quality of life. There are numerous examples of such a causal link, for example ADB data to demonstrate that educated farmers have larger and better crops. However, in poor rural areas, it is not easy to convince people that short-term foregone earning while receiving education will be more than compensated for by becoming literate and/or educated. This is particularly so for girls' education.

- How does a project provide a real demonstration of the link between education and/or literacy and the attainment of a better life?
- There is a need for good role models to demonstrate this link, Projects need to examine alternative ways of providing such models; for example, soap operas, cartoons, respected figures, etc.
- How can the project convince the community that girls' education has a social and economic benefit?

4.Internal versus external motivation to carry out the project

The sustainability of a project depends very much on the motivation of its players. When a project is implemented from outside, local community members must be convinced by some means to want to be involved. The difficulty of this will depend to a large extent on their involvement and feelings of ownership. The following are relevant factors:

- Internal motivation to implement and continue the project will be more successful at sustaining the project than external rewards.
- How can the project inculcate internal motivation?
- Can the project establish pride or reduction of "loss of face" through its activities?
- Can a feeling of ownership of the project be established at the local level?
- Is there a perception of direct benefits (social and economic) from the project? . If external incentives and rewards are used in the early stages of implementation, how is motivation later internalised?

5.The possibility of local cultures, values, taboos, customs and language being undermined or destroyed.

A number of the projects target ethnic minority groups while in other cases teachers and project personnel often come from outside the local community, In all cases, literacy is applied to the national language rather than the local one. In addition, attitudes and values of teachers and project personnel are usually different from those of the local community. Given the important link between language and cultural identity, the issue of "literate in which language?' needs to be raised. Economic, political, social and cultural factors all play a role in this matter. However, it is worth mentioning as an example that

Papua New Guinea (a country of 4 million with hundreds of linguistic groups) has just introduced educational reforms which have resulted in a system of a 3 year vernacular language elementary education followed by 5 years of primary education in the national tongue. Thus, the following questions should be addressed:

— Is the model of education (teaching and learning) being introduced to local (ethnic) communities appropriate to the needs of the local community? . Who decides what is needed? Do the expressed needs of the community impact on the project goals and activities?

— What is an appropriate balance between cultural values of the local communities and those of the nation as a whole?

— How do local concerns have influence (should they?) when wider national provincial policies (for example, of globalisation) are being pursued? . For ethnic minorities, will literacy training in the national language threaten the existence of the local language (and thus identity and culture)?

Project analysis

Participants of the meeting worked in sub groups to analyse the reports of country experiences in order to identify major impacts, successful strategies, problems and possible strategies for future implementation. A matrix was used as a framework for this analysis. The matrix analysed the project in terms of the following dimensions:

— Policy

— Access, enrolment and learning achievement
— Teachers
— Curriculum materials
— Social and cultural context
— Facilities
— Parents and the community
— Project management
— The project as a model intervention.

Major impacts and successes of the projects

Policy: Impacts

— All participating countries are committed to EFA to achieve universalisation of primary education
— Funding: own sources, loans, aids
— Decentralised planning
— Curriculum development
— National curricular framework and within that, local, need-based, group-specific curriculum development, textbooks and learning materials based on:
  — the experiences of the child
  — a gender sensitive curriculum
  — a rural orientation
  — changes in education policies of the project states/ provinces.

Policy: Successes

— decentralisation

— grassroots implementation

— commitment of local leaders and local policy makers

— building commitment and greater understanding among policy makers and administrative staff at all levels

Access, Enrolment and Learning Achivements: Impacts

— out-of-school children, particularly girls, commenced schooling

— a pleasant learning environment with interesting learning materials were developed

— school activities were based on children' s experiences and lives

— the environment was girl friendly

— a greater link between the school and the community was established

Access, Enrolment and Learning Achivements: Successes

— a special focus on accessing education to deprived groups

— enrolment drives and household census

— special incentives for girls and disadvantaged groups

— prizes for teachers/villagers who introduce children, especially girls, to school

— encouraging girls for active participation in the classroom and in outdoor activities . making boys and girls share leadership and work in school as co-partners.

Teahchers: Impacts

— better qualification

— competency based training

— moral motivation

— different approaches for teacher training adopted

— incentives for teachers to realise UPE

— adding a broad vision and new competencies

— supplementing with local experts

— gender training for teachers.

Teahchers: Successes

— different approaches for teacher training

— incentives for teachers to realise UPE

— orientation for special groups, girls and disadvantaged groups

— mobile teacher training

— resource centres based on school clusters or at sub-district level for in-service teacher training.

Curriculum Materials: Impacts

— related to education and work

— develop locally based curriculum/materials

— skills development for income generation programs

— gender inclusive learning materials

Curriculum Materials: Successes

— developed locally based curriculum materials

— income generation program skills developed

— development of curriculum, training modules and training materials for gender sensitisation of all educational personnel

— development of campaign materials, posters, songs, audio tapes, video films, etc.

Social and Cultural Context: Impacts

— breaking down inhibitions against female education

— economic betterment of women/girls

— improved family conditions

— improved self confidence, self esteem and self reliance

— mass mobilisation

Social and Cultural Context: Successes

— teacher orientation for special groups

— gender inclusive teaching and learning

— textbooks free of gender bias

— advocacy and mass mobilisation about the importance of education of girls and women

Facilities: Impacts and Successes

— increased number of NFE centres and schools

— better and more permanent school buildings

— vocational facilities (equipment, tools, training materials) established

— attached to schools are mini-farms (fish, vegetables, animals, tree plantations, fruit trees)

— construction of toilets and bathrooms with a proper water supply

— reduced travel distance to NFE centres and schools

— revolving fund for skills development and income generation created

— school activities (eg., VAC) which generate income for educational use

— a more attractive environment in schools (especially important for girls)

— better home environment

— community willing to provide space/house for NFE classes

— demand for community infrastructure (water, electricity, etc.) established

— greater access to learning which subsequently leads to improvements in family

— planning practices, health, sanitation, nutrition, environment, and control of diseases such as malaria

— reduction of drop-out rate

- reduction of barriers for girls' access to schools leading to increased participation and retention rates for girls
- reinforcing parents' commitment for their children' s education because of better facilities
- school and NFE centres become community development centres.

Parents and Community: Impacts and Successes

- favourable attitude towards education
- increasing number of learners and better attendance
- literacy leading to skills development and their application leading to increased per capita income
- support to teachers is increased (better communication between teachers and the community)
- parents help to train and impart local skills and knowledge
- community contribution (in cash, labour, materials etc.) to improve and protect the physical facilities
- increased request for more education and health facilities
- increased assertiveness
- increased role of women in social and economic life
- more involvement by the community in selecting teachers for training formal signing of local contracts
- committing parents to send their children to school

Management: Impact

- management structure established at all levels (better interaction and communication) with a single coordination committee at the central level
- the central level provides the goal (and in some cases, also the action plan) for the project
- the central level provides a monitoring and evaluation mechanism local level participation in management of the project (in some cases, at all levels while in others only for local aspects)
- the central level controls the funding of the project (in some cases, the distribution of funds is determined centrally, in other cases according to local requests)
- revolving funds and school profits from income generation activities are managed at the local level (eg., school management boards and village committees)
- strengthening resource centres at the local level
- training of trainers
- a feedback mechanism has been established at all levels

The Project as a whole : Impact

- As a good model for implementation of EFA

Major problems and bottlenecks of projects

Policy

- lack of commitment by local leaders and senior administrators

— isolation of primary schools

— lack of coordination,

— lack of project management skills

— shortage of funds

— small local allocation to primary education in national budget

— lack of networking

Access, Enrolment and Learning Acheivements

— lack of schools/learning centres (low supply)

— social and cultural barriers, and domestic work-load (low demand)

— inadequate teaching and learning leads to failure and dropout

— uninteresting school environment and learning materials, lack ofjoyful activities

Teachers

— lack of appropriate competencies and motivation

— lack of information and opportunities for professional development

— lack of female teachers and principals

Curriculum materials

— one localised curriculum cannot be easily used in another place

— lack of a responsive curriculum

Facilities

— meeting the new demand for more facilities within the context of existing capital and human resource constraints

— sustainability

— effective and efficient use of existing facilities

— security and vandalism

— inadequate matching of facilities' provision and use to the demands of the agricultural cycle inappropriate location of schools and NFE centres (political versus educational decisions)

Parents and Community

— lack of awareness of the benefits of education

— heterogeneity in culture, religion, traditions, language and dialect

— poverty alleviation through literacy and education is not strong

— literacy program does not match the agricultural cycle

— lack of teachers and instructors from the local community

— medium of instruction or content (or both) is in a second language

— low involvement of NGOs and local community leaders

— natural disasters or geographical location makes education a low priority

Management

— communication with UNESCO NATCOMs and the implementing project

— organisation is very poor (Viet Nam is an exception). Slow budget release and allocation creates difficulties for project implementation

— lack of integration between project goals and plans of action of the UNESCO project with those of national policies

— a detailed schedule of budget allocation and required milestones over the full life of the project is not available. This hinders a more logical implementation to be planned

— no regular and timely supervision by supervisors

— lack of appropriate management skills

The project as a whole

— others (in- and out-of-country) want to copy and implement the project model but do not have the resources, skills and knowledge to do this

Future strategies to improve the project

Participants of the meeting worked in sub-groups to identify possible strategies for future implementation. These strategies were linked to the problems and bottlenecks which are preventing the projects from currently achieving all of their objectives. The same framework for analysis was used. This matrix analysed the project in terms of the following dimensions:

— Policy

— Access, enrolment and learning achievement

— Teachers

— Curriculum materials

— Social and cultural context

— Facilities

— Parents and the community

— Project management

— The project as a model intervention

The results of this analysis are presented below:

Policy

— implementation of public campaigns especially for local leaders, NGOs, and women' s (youth) groups

— building awareness and commitment among policy makers, planners, and administrators via orientation programs

— implementation of inter-departmental coordination for potential support agencies

— unproved organisation (personnel and regulations) at different administrative levels

— mobilising funds

— implementation of management training for project personnel (es., planning, database training, coordination, monitoring, and evaluation)

— networking and collaborative mechanisms

— increased sharing of information, expertise and materials

Access, enrolment and learning achievements

— expand access with formal and non-formal educational programs

— continue mass campaigns in local communities for enrolment and participation

— provision of incentives and motivation for poor girls and boys

— provision of incentives for families, especially mothers, to support their daughters during schooling

— ensure quality improvement of classroom interactions, and school activities

— introduction of flexible school calendars

— carry out innovative studies in learning achievement, not only in language maths but also in social ability, attitudes etc.

— ensuring that education is a joyful experience with more attractive and relevant activities

Teahcers

— improve teachers' competencies by well designed training programs

— stimulate and maintain their motivation and commitment by means of professional, spiritual and material rewards

— establish resource networks for teachers

— involve teachers in on-going pedagogic studies

— train teachers on life skills

— arrange teacher visits to successful project sites

— orient teachers to adapt the national curriculum to local conditions

— train teachers to develop low cost teaching aids

Curriculum Materials

— exchange of materials to avoid duplication

— development of a needs-based curriculum

— materials should be locally specific and be community based

— development of a curriculum which is functional and based on daily life

Social and cultural contexts

— preparation of girls and women for leadership, decision making roles and political participation

— creation of a culture of self reliance and a positive self image

Facilities

— the sustainability of the program activities, after completion of the pilot project, should be considered and an effective action plan for sustainability included.(eg., on-going maintenance of school buildings)

— encourage and involve the local community to explore the different ways and means of best utilising the school or NFE centre facilities (eg., to conduct community meetings)

— create an awareness through orientation programs (ownership of school and/or NFE centre facilities by the community). Involve the community in the building of school facilities (eg., through labour and materials provision)

— conduct a survey on innovative alternatives for providing education and literacy to farmers

— carry out school and community mapping to assist in the optimal location of schools and NFE centres

Parents and community

— carry out extensive advocacy and promotional campaigns on the benefits of education implement a multicultural approach to moral and values education, in textbooks, campaigns and instruction, to create harmony and unity provision of training and other incentives for qualified local community people.

— priority should be given for local people to be selected for teacher training experts to carry out research for improving the medium of instruction and content of education and literacy programs involve NGOs and community leaders from the planning stage rather than only at later stages.

— UNESCO and NATCOMs to review their current procedures of communication UNESCO to provide, at the beginning of the pilot project, a detailed schedule of budget allocation and required milestones over the full life of the project. This will allow a more logical implementation to be planned provision of training to highlight the importance of regular and timely supervision

— both UNESCO and governments to investigate a mechanism for improved integration of plans of action

— provision of inter-country visits and management courses funded by UNESCO, both in-country and abroad . the project cycle to be for 5 years rather than 3 years (because of the cycle of primary education)

The project as a whole

— UNESCO, in conjunction with national governments, should act as a broker to explore funding from donor agencies for expansion of project activities

6

Non-Formal Education in India

In India, the National Policy on Education (NPE), 1986 and the Programme of Action 1992 envisage a large systematic programme of Non-formal Education (NFE) for those who cannot attend the full day schools. It assumes that if the essential requirements for running a good programme are fulfilled, NFE can result in provision of education comparable in quality with formal schooling. It visualises NFE as child-centred, environment-oriented system to meet the diverse needs of comparatively deprived sections of society. Decentralised community participation through Village Education Committees (VECs) in planning, running, and overseeing the NFE programme has been considered crucial for its success.

Although the focus of the programme is on the educationally backward States, it also covers urban slums, hilly, tribal and desert areas and projects for education of working children in other States/UTs as well. The programme is implemented through State/ UT Governments as well as NGOs. The Central assistance to

States/UTs is being provided on sharing basis between the Central Government and the State Governments in the ratio of 60:40 for co-educational centres and administrative resource support and 90: 10 for exclusively girls' centres. Hundred per cent Central assistance is being provided to NGOs for running NFE Centres and Experimental and Innovative Projects. The programme of NFE is being monitored through Quarterly Progress Reports (QPRs), periodic evaluations conducted by Joint Evaluation Teams (JETs) and field visits of Central and State Government officials. On the basis of the feedback received, remedial action is being taken for effective implementation of the programme. Operations Research Group (ORG), New Delhi has also been asked to develop tools for evaluation of the programme along with the schemes of Teacher Education and Operation Blackboard.

Currently, 740 voluntary agencies are implementing NFE programme in 25 States/ UTs. Another 85 agencies have been sanctioned 9,485 NFE centres in the current year. Effort to make the programme more meaningful is being taken up and experiences of successful NFE programme of organisations such as Lok Jumbish, Shiksha Karmi, etc. are being taken into consideration while revising the scheme. The overall aim of the scheme is to promote experimentation and innovation for the achievement of goals spelt out in the National Policy on Education. The scheme has been in operation from the year 1987-88. Under the scheme voluntary organisations are given 100 per cent grants for trying out innovative strategies that could be replicated/ disseminated in the formal stream. Main areas of experimentation and innovations have been: action research, community mobilisation, curriculum designing and preparation of need-based teaching-learning materials and aids, training of personnel and development of teaching techniques, new evaluation methods, linkage of school education with vocational education and alternative method of education for special target groups such as, disabled children, girls, working children, tribal children, etc. Currently, 45 voluntary agencies are implementing the programme. Some of the leading agencies are MV Foundation, Secunderabad working on education of child labour, Deccan Development.

Since its inception two decades ago, the NFE programme has consistently grown in size and coverage. In particular, significant expansion of the programme took place during 1990s in terms of number of NFE centres and the number of children enrolled in them. The strategy of NFE is as follows:

— Condensed course of about two years' duration.

— Part-time instructions at a time/place convenient to learners in small groups.

— Part-time honorary instructor /supervisor locally recruited and trained.

— Emphasis on flexibility and decentralisation of management.

— Use of curriculum and teaching-learning material comparable to the formal system and relevant to local environment and learner's needs.

— Testing and certification of NFE students to enable their entry into formal system.

By 1997, there were 279,000 NFE centres covering about 7 million children in 21 States. Of these, 240,747 are being run by State Governments and 37,808 by 544 NGOs/ Voluntary Agencies. Five States, viz., Uttar Pradesh,

Bihar, Andhra Pradesh, Madhya Pradesh and Orissa account for 81 percent of NFE centres. The spread of NFE programme is moderate in Rajasthan and Assam. Coverage is very limited in Jammu and Kashmir, and NorthEastern States; the programme started in Arunachal Pradesh during 1990s.

The NFE programme emphasis on implementation through local and national NGOs/Voluntary Agencies. Government of India has been giving liberal grants to support such activities by NGOs. Participation of voluntary agencies in NFE has increased phenomenally during 1990s. While there were 7310 NFE centres run by voluntary agencies in 1993, their number swelled to 37,808 in 1996 and to 58788 in 1999. Besides running NFE centres, these NGOs have been implementing 41 experimental and innovative programmes for promoting elementary education. The number of NGOs participating in NFE has been increasing during 1990s. Over the years, the NFE scheme has given rise to a number of innovative experiments by NGOs as well as other implementing agencies.

Almost all the major EFA projects have evolved different approaches and institutional arrangements for reaching primary education to the disadvantaged within the broad framework of NFE. Some of these are the 'Sahaj Siksha programme' under Lok Jumbish in Rajasthan and the Alternate School Programme under DPEP in Madhya Pradesh. This aspect of the scope provided by NFE for promoting pluralism and variety in design and delivery of primary education needs further attention from policy makers and planners. During 1990s, two features of the NFE programme were stressed. These were importance of making necessary investments in qualitative improvement of NFE, and reiteration that the advantages of NFE lay in its flexibility and adaptability to the needs of disadvantaged children. Evaluation of the NFE programme has also made several useful suggestions for streamlining the organisation of the NFE scheme, improving infra-structure, qualitative improvement in various inputs and their monitoring with a view to increasing the internal efficiency of the NFE system and enhancing its effectiveness. These factors have to be further strengthened during the years to come.

NFE is a low cost alternative to formal primary school. However, findings of evaluation of the scheme do not lend support to this assumption. The revised programme of NFE has to aim at delivering "literacy, numeracy and awareness" to those out-of-school children who can not be brought to the formal education system and not cost saving. This approach places a greater challenge on the government for raising adequate resources for the NFE programme. Despite numerous difficulties encountered and challenges faced, it cannot be denied that NFE has provided access to primary education for millions of children in remote and inaccessible rural areas and urban slums, specially girls and the disadvantaged sections of the society. In that sense the contribution of NFE in EFA is substantial and significant.

NFE Alternates for Children-out-of-school

According to 1991 census, there are 11.28 million child workers (6.18 million boys and 5.10 million girls) in the age group 5-14. About 91 percent of these children are concentrated in the rural areas. Of the 11.28 million working children, 9.08 millions are classified as main workers and another 2.2 million are classified as marginal workers. Besides, nearly 7 million children are enumerated as involved in house-hold duties. It may be noted here that 6.2 millions (88 per cent) of these are girls. Household duties could mean anything from assisting in the family farm or any other family occupation besides taking care of household chores like cooking, taking care of children, fetching water, fuel and so on. Thus, if a comprehensive definition of work is taken, the total incidence of child workers is quite substantial and merit serious attention when progress towards EFA is being assessed. Action Plan for Dealing with the Problem India has all along followed a proactive policy in the matter of tackling the problem of child labour.

The Indian Constitution requires the State to protect children against being forced by economic necessity to enter vocations unsuited to their age and strength. However, it should be recognized that the problem of working children and their education can not be treated only as a responsibility of the Labour or Education Department. It is a multi-sectoral problem having a direct interface with several other areas of social and economic policy making. these factors in view and in pursuance of the constitutional mandate, the government adopted the National Policy on Child Labour in 1987. The Policy which forms the framework of action with respect to the problem of child labour comprise a legislative action plan, focussing on general development programmes for benefiting children wherever possible and project-based action plans in areas of high concentration of child labour engaged in wage/quasi-wage employment. These action plans together with the recommendations of the National

Policy on Education – 1986 for the bases for initiating programmes for education of the working children. Major Action Initiated in Recent Years Following the National Policy on Child Labour and the National Policy on Education, several new initiatives have been taken for reaching basic education to the working children. From several angles, the intensity of action both through media campaigns and innovative educational programmes has been at a high pitch. There is no doubt that this has been considerably influenced by the intense debates and consultations that have taken place at the international level in the last couple of decades including the adoption of the Convention of Child Rights to which India is a signatory.

In India, twelve National Child Labour Projects have been initiated in areas of high concentration of child labour. These include: Andhra Pradesh (Jaggampet and Markapur), Bihar (Garwah), Madhya Pradesh (Mandsaur), Maharashtra (Thane), Orissa (Smbalpur), Rajasthan (Jaipur), Tamil Nadu (Sivakasi), and Uttar Pradesh (Varanasi-Mirzapur-Bhadohi, Moradabad, Aligarh and Ferozabad). A major activity undertaken under the NCLP is the establishment of special schools to provide non-formal education, vocational training, supplementary nutrition, stipend and health care to children withdrawn from employment. About 85 child labour projects have been sanctioned in child labour endemic states covering about 130,000 children. The Government has approved continuation of the project and increase in the number of Projects to 100.

Recognizing the problems of implementation involved and the need for inter-ministerial coordination, a Central Monitoring Committee has been set up under the Chairmanship of Secretary, Ministry of Labour. The

Committee which has representatives of child labour endemic states and other concerned national ministries is vested with the responsibility for overall supervision, monitoring and evaluation of the projects. Under the Grants-in-Aid scheme of the Ministry of Labour, NGOs are being financially assisted to the extent of 75 per cent of the Project cost for taking up welfare projects for working children where they are provided with non-formal education, supplementary nutrition, health care and vocational/skill training. During 1998-99, 83 NGOs participated in the programme involving a grant of more than Rs. 9 million.

In addition, the Ministry of Human Resource Development also provides financial assistance to NGOs involved in education of the working children. In fact, 1990s have seen the emergence of several innovative programmes in the non-government sector for dealing with the problem of providing basic education to working children. Within the education sector, all the major EFA projects have specific components to meet the education needs of the working children. Special attention is paid to the needs of the girl child who is deprived of schooling due to involvement in domestic work and is often not counted as a working child.

Several government ans well as NGO led innovative education programmes are established in the country to educate the poor children Some of them are:

i) *National Bal Bhavan (NBB)*: The National Bal Bhavan, New Delhi was established by the Government of India in 1956 at the initiative of Pandit Jawahar Lal Nehru. An autonomous institution fully funded by the Department of Education, the NBB has been contributing towards enhancing the creativity amongst children in the age-group 5-16 years especially from the weaker sections of the society. The children can pursue activities of their choice such as creative arts, performing arts, environment, astronomy, photography, integrated activities, physical activities, science-related activities, etc. in a joyful manner. The programmes are so designed as to explore the inner potential of a child and give him opportunities for expression of ideas through various media. Bal Bhavan thus aims at the all-round growth of a child in a free and happy atmosphere and helps them develop a scientific temper.

ii) Nutritional Support to Primary Education: This programme is popularly known as the Mid-day Meals Scheme, was launched on 15 August 1995 on a nationwide scale. This programme intends to give a boost to the universalisation of primary education by increasing enrolment, retention and attendance and to improve the nutritional status of students in, the primary classes (I-V). From 1997-98 onwards, the programme has covered all the children studying in primary classes in the Government, local body and government-aided schools. This is one of the largest school nutrition programmes in the world today.

The total number of beneficiaries at present being covered is estimated to be 9.75 crore in nearly 6.88 lakh schools in all the blocks and urban areas in the country. The programme is much successful wherein cooked meals/processed food is being served. The Central support under this programme is on provision of foodgrains free of cost to the implementing agencies for which economic cost is reimbursed to the Food Corporation of India and reimbursement of transportation cost to district authorities for moving foodgrains from Food Corporation of India godowns to schools /villages.

iii) *Shiksha Karmi Project* (SKP): This Project was launched in 1987 on the basis of agreement signed between Swedish International Development Cooperation Agency (SIDA) and the Government of India. Phase I of the project was up to 30 June 1994. According to the specific agreement between the Government of India and the Government of Sweden, Phase II of the SKP was up to June 1997 which was subsequently extended to June 1998. During Phase I, SIDA and the Government of Rajasthan shared expenditure in the ratio of 9:1, respectively. During Phase II the cost-sharing between SIDA and the Government of Rajasthan was revised in the proportion of 50:50. Provision for the SIDA's share has been made in the Central Plan Budget which was subsequently reimbursable by SIDA on the basis of actual expenditure incurred by the Rajasthan Shiksha Karmi Board (RSKB) through which the Shiksha Karmi Project is being implemented. The project aims at universalisation and qualitative improvement of primary education in remote and socio -economically backward villages in Rajasthan with primary attention given to girls. The project identifies teacher absenteeism as a major obstacle in achieving the goal of Universalisation of Elementary Education (UEE).

A primary school in remote villages, with the teacher not residing there, often tended to become dysfunctional, and parents as well as children failed to relate to such an institution, leading to high dropout rates. Under SKP, regular teachers are replaced by local teachers who are less qualified but specially trained. A Shiksha Karmi (SK) is a local person with minimum educational qualification of Class VIII for men and Class V for women. To overcome the basic lack of qualification, Shiksha Karmis are given intensive training through induction programme as well as periodic refresher courses. The project is being implemented by the Government of Rajasthan through Rajasthan Shiksha Karmi Board (RSKB) with the assistance of voluntary agencies. The RSKB has a Governing Council and an Executive Council. These bodies are represented through two representatives of this Department.

NGOs and the community play a pivotal role in the implementation of the Shiksha Karmi Project. The Village Education Committees (VECs) have contributed to the improvement of school environment, augmentation of infrastructure and facilities, larger enrolment of children through school mapping and micro-planning in the Shiksha Karmi schools. Enrolment of girls, their attendance and retention in primary schools is one of the serious challenges in achieving Universalisation of Elementary Education in Rajasthan.

SKP aims at addressing these through decentralised initiatives involving the community. At the grassroot level, Panchayat Samities, Shiksha Karmi Sahyogis, subject specialists of NGOs, Shiksha Karmis and the village community constantly interact with each other to achieve the aims of the project. Prehar Pathshalas (PPs) (school of convenient timings) under the SKP provide educational programmes for out-of-school children who cannot attend regular day schools due to their preoccupation at home and in other work. In PPs condensed formal school curriculum and learning materials are followed. At present 22,359 girls who constitute 71 per cent of learners in PPs are benefiting from this facility. Under the innovative and experimental activities, Angan Pathshalas have proved effective in attracting girls to primary schools. Mahila Sahyogis have confirmed their utility in motivating girls to attend schools/PPs in difficult areas. Integration of children with partial disabilities in day schools and PPs have been attempted on a pilot basis.

SKP has emerged as a unique instrument of human resource development. It has enabled rural youth with inherent talent and potential to blossom into confident para-professlionals with self-respect and dignity. A significant number of children covered by the SK schools are from among SCs/STs. There has been six-fold increase in the enrolment of children in the schools taken over by the project.

Scheme for Assistance to Voluntarv agencies for non-formal Education for elementary age-group children under the Programme of Universalisation of Elementary Education

In compliance of the Directive contained in Article 45 of the Constitution, the National Policy on Education 1986(NPE) accords an unqualified priority to Universalisation of Elementary Education (UEE). NPE declares that by 1990 all children who attain the age of about 11 years will have had five years of schooling, or its equivalent through the non-formal stream and, likewise, by 1995 all children upto 14 years of age will be provided free and compulsory education. Effort will be made to enrol children in 6-14 age-group in schools, but NPE acknowledges that it may not be possible to provide primary schools in all habitations, and it would also be unrealistic to expect working children and girls, who attend to their siblings and are engaged in other domestic chores, to attend whole-day schools. It is, therefore, envisaged that a large and systematic programme of non-formal education will be launched for these children. NPE goes on to say that while Government will take overall responsibility for planning and implementation of the non-formal education programme, much of the work of running of NFE centres will be done through voluntary agencies and Panchayati Raj Institutions. Recognising that, in the past, voluntary agencies have not been able to play their due role, the NPE directs that obstacle to their participation will be removed.

The Programme of Action (POA) for implementation of NPE spells out, in a somewhat greater detail, the strategy to be adopted for implementation of the new programme of non-formal education. The salient characteristics of non-formal education envisaged in POA are:

— *Flexibility* in regard to admission requirements, duration, timing etc.

— *Relevance* of curriculum and instructional methods;

— *Diversification* in the type of course to be offered and its supplementation by vocational education; and

— *Decentralisation* in management structure and financial powers.

The implications of the approach spelt out in NPE and POA on the curricular aspects of NFE have been further examined. Essential features of the curricula and teaching/learning materials proposed to be used by children will be their relevance to the needs, work life and environment of the learners. Curriculum and learning materials will, however, be developed keeping in view the expected learning outcomes and in particular, the required level of learning envisaged in NPE as a feature of National System of Education. The expected learning outcomes would serve as the reference points for the evaluation of learners enrolled in non-formal education centres. This would ensure that pupils in NFE system also get proper certification for their achievements and are enabled to take advantage of multi-point entry facilities in regular full-time schools at appropriate stages.

Under the new programme of NFE, efforts will be made to evolve different models of non-formal education programmes. The agencies implementing the programme will be encouraged to design and adopt the most suitable model depending upon the requirements of the target groups, the kind of expertise available with them, the support system etc. An illustrative model indicating cost parameters is given in Annex-II. However, NFE programmes should be designed in such a way that they confirm to the overall objectives spelt out in NPE and POA.

There is need for a substantial strengthening of the supervisory and administrative apparatus of NFE. Rather than depending on the urban-oriented bureaucratic model, emphasis should be laid on taking up well designed project of approximately 100 NFE centres, to be taken up in a compact and contiguous area. Supervisors should be selected from the local community, if possible an experienced and committed NFE Instructor. These persons should be intensively trained and where possible also involve an organisation of continuing education programme. Village Education Committees should be set up as envisaged in NPE/POA to involve the local community in the programme and also to make the NFE centre incharge accountable to it.

Objectives

The broad aim of the scheme is to effectively involve voluntary agencies, public trusts, non-profit making companies, social activist groups etc., in the implementation of non-formal education programme for the elementary age-group children. Within this overall aim, the specific objectives of the scheme are as follows:

— To develop the programme of non-formal education for meeting the educational needs of out-of-school children;

— To establish a partnership between the government on the one hand and voluntary agencies, public trust, non-profit making companies, social activist groups, etc. on the other, in the great task of provision of educational opportunities for children who cannot enrol themselves in whole-day schools;

— To demonstrate through adoption in the field various alternative models that can be adopted for UEE.

— To identify from the local community young persons and to train them as organisers of NFE centres and as community workers.

— To give special attention to the training of women non-formal education organisers for furtherance of the objectives of women's development as envisaged in NPE; and

— To evolve curricula, learning materials, instructional methods, evaluation techniques etc., relevant to the needs, environment and working life of the learners.

Eligibility

7. (a) Registered voluntary societies, public trusts and non-profit making companies would be eligible for assistance under this scheme. Ordinarily, agencies which are not legal entities would not be eligible. However, even agencies and social activist groups which are not legal entities may be considered for assistance provided the Collector/Deputy Commissioner certifies regarding the practical difficulties owing to which they could not be registered and regarding the bonafides of such organisations. In respect of projects taken up for abolition of child labour or for amelioration of the condition of working children, autonomous bodies set up by the Central or State Governments will also be eligible for assistance under this scheme.

(b) In exceptional cases, a registered society or a public trust fulfilling requirements as an eligible agency may be given assistance for mobilisation, involvement and provision of financial support to other voluntary agencies, social activist groups and individuals.

(c) In order to be eligible for financial assistance under this scheme an agency should:-

- have a proper constitution or articles of association;
- have a properly constituted managing body with its powers and duties clearly defined in the constitution;
- be in a position to secure the involvement, on voluntary basis, of knowledgeable persons for furtherance of its programmes;
- not be run for the profit of any individual or a body of individuals;
- not discriminate against any person or group of persons on the ground of sex, religion, caste or creed;
- not in any manner incite communal disharmony;
- not proselytise and eschew violence.

(d) Only those eligible agencies which have been in existence for 3 years would be considered for assistance under this scheme. The requirement may be waived in respect of agencies with specially qualified workers or which can be otherwise jusify a special consideration

Nature and extent of assistance

8 (a) Eligible agencies will be given grants on a cent per cent basis for non-formal education both at the primary and middle stages. Specific activities for which grants may be given would include.

- running of non-formal education centres in the field, along with costs involved in supervision and management;

— non-formalisation of the formal education system;

— activities to explore linkage between NFE and formal education;

— resource, development including development of curricula, teaching/learning material, development and production of instructional aids, development of evaluation techniques etc; and

— management expenses essential for action under paragraph 7(b).

(b) Grants under this scheme will be given to voluntary agencies working in the educationally backward States, namely, Andhra Pradesh, Assam, Bihar, Jammu & Kashmir, Madhya Pradesh, Orissa, Rajasthan, Uttar Pradesh and West Bengal. In the remaining States also eligible agencies would be provided assistance if their work is in –

— hilly areas,

— predominantly tribal areas known for educational backwardness, and

— urban slums.

Eligible agencies and autonomous bodies set up by Government will also be eligible for assistance as described above in projects for working children in all parts of the country.

(c) Assistance may be sought for such duration as the applicant agency may consider appropriate. Ordinarily, such assistance will be provided on a long term basis, but not exceeding the balance of a Five Year Plan period at a time. Indication in regard to the period for which grant has been approved would normally be given in the letter of sanction.

The Procedure

9.(a) *Applicaton* : Any agency eligible to receive assistance may make an application in the form appended hereto. The applications should be addressed to the Ministry of H.R.D.(Department of Education), Government of India, New Delhi through the State Education Department (with a copy endorsed directly to the Ministry). The State Government should give its views, within a period of three months, regarding the agency's eligibility, suitability, relevance of the proposal and the capacity of the agency to implement it, etc. Comments should be sent to the State Government even if the proposal is not recommended, giving reasons therefor. Application for extension of the project will not be required to be sent through the State Government. It would, however, be necessary for the voluntary agency to send a copy of its request for extension of the project to the State Government by *Registered A/D* post. All-India organisations may make applications directly to the Ministry.

(b) *Grant-in-Aid Committee* : The applications for grant-in-aid would be considered by a Grant-in-Aid Committee to be appointed by the Ministry. Ordinarily, the Committee will go by the advice of the State Government. However, in the event of the State Government not making any recommendations, or while considering cases in departure from the advice of the State Government and, if necessary also of the agency making application, the representative of the State Govts. and/or Voluntary Agency will be invited to discuss the proposal with the Committee.

(c) *Release of Grant* : On approval of the Project the grant shall be released to the agency on an annual basis in two instalments – the first one shall be released immediately after the issue of the sanction. After the agency concerned has utilised 75% of an instalment, it may make a request for release of the subsequent instalment along with a progress report and statement of expenditure. Release of grants in the second and subsequent years will be made on a similar basis, provided that before release of the second instalment in a particular financial year (beginning with the second year), the utilisation certificate and audited statement in respect of the grants released till the end of the preceding year shall be furnished.

(d) *Disbursement* : Grants for programmes undertaken by Government institutions will be provided to the State Government/Union Territory Administration according to the normal procedure. Grant payable to a voluntary agency, public trust, non-profit making company etc., would be remitted to it directly by a demand draft/cheque drawn in its favour by the Ministry of Human Resource Development.

Conditions of Grant

The grant-receiving agency will be required to execute a bond on a prescribed form. The bond should be supported by two sureties if the agency is not a legal entity.

An agency in receipt of financial assistance shall be open to inspection by an officer of the Union Ministry of Human Resource Development/ or National Council of Educational Research and Training or the State Education Department.

The accounts of the project shall be maintained properly and separately and submitted as and when required. They should be open to check by an officer deputed by the Government of India or the State Government. They shall also be opened to a test check by the Comptroller and Auditor General of India at his discretion.

The audited accounts together with the utilisation certificate in the prescribed form duly counter-signed by the Chartered Accountants are required to be furnished within six months in respect of a preceding year or after expiry of the duration for which grant is approved.

The agency shall maintain a record of all assets acquired wholly or substantially out of Government grant and maintain a register of such assets in the prescribed proforma. Such assets shall not be disposed of, encumbered or utilised for purposes other than those for which the grant was given, without prior sanction of the Government of India. Should the agency cease to exist at any time, such properties shall revert to the Government of India.

When the State Government/Government of India have reasons to believe that the sanctioned money is not being utilised for approved purposes the payment of grant may be stopped and the earlier grants recovered.

The institution must exercise reasonable economy in the working of the approved project.

The grantee agency shall furnish to the Ministry of Human Resource Development reports as may be prescribed.

The decisions of the Secretary to the Government of India in the Ministry of Human Resource Development, Department of Education on the question whether there has been breach or violation of any of the terms and conditions mentioned in the sanction letter shall be final and binding on the grantee.

7

Contributions of Non-formal Education

Today, 125 million primary school-age children are not in school; most of them are girls. Another 150 million children start primary school but drop out before they have completed four years of education, the vast majority before they have acquired basic literacy skills. In much of the developing world the education provided to children is of abysmal quality. The right of the world's children to an education remains one of the most widely and systematically violated of all human rights.

Educatioinal agencies have become extremely concerned about the limitations of the post-Jomtien efforts to achieve EFA, there is a danger that the discussion about educational development is reduced to the basic question of how do we get more "bums on seats" in conventional classrooms. For the sake of the future of millions of children, the debate must be as much on the nature and quality of the education that is provided as on access per se. In fact, a more pervasive discussion on what constitutes the essence of quality basic education for children and youngsters could also affect our efforts to promote participation in such education.

A "bums on seats" debate avoids the significance of the statistical presentation of "participation in primary education" as the number of children attending conventional primary schooling, as throughout the post-Jomtien years the primary school has been regarded as the main institution responsible for the provision of basic education for children. In the same vein, all the benefits usually associated with education have been assumed to apply only to this type of provision. This presentation has evaded thorough discussions on what "basic education" goes on outside the schools that may be worthy of recognition. Moreover, it tends to downplay questions about what goes on in these institutions and why it is that so many parents have difficulties in letting their children go to school.

In all likelihood large numbers of children will continue to be barred from primary education, in the standard definition, as they may not have the most basic resources necessary to acquire basic education through "normal" schooling, or have other essential social or economic obligations preventing them from spending a major part of the day at school (or traveling to and from), or decide (or be told by their parents) that what is on offer is not relevant in relation to what is expected. Beyond this problematic of demand there is the issue of the extent to which countries and communities can afford to produce the kind of physical and human school environment that is considered standard. Foreign assistance cannot be the driving force upon which all plans are to be based—as is actually proposed.

The inability to provide quality education for all in accordance with established prescriptions compels us foremost to rethink the premises upon which the present education system is based and re-negotiate with learners and communities what basic education should be all about and how it should be provided. It constitutes a challenge to take the "expanded vision" of Jomtien further and explore systematically how the limitations of the existing formal school system can be transcended through explicit recognition of the environment in which education is to take place. This implies greater sensitivity to both to the needs and interests of communities and to the conditions under which education for all can be ensured.

In the process an explicit distinction needs to be made between what is to be learned and how and where the learning is provided. It is in this context that the strengths and weaknesses of alternative opportunities for learning, including NFE provisions, can be re-examined.

An expanded vision of the Jomtien agenda would now, more than any time, take cognizance of a number of premises that impact on what is to be offered, how, and under what conditions. The main premises can be presented as follows.

There is a diversity among learners, including among children in the school going age-group, in terms of:

— *social and economic circumstances*: There is an increasing number of children who have social and/ or economic obligations—some of which are not new, some of which are—such as children having to look after siblings as a result of HIV/Aids.

— *learning needs.* This refers not only to children requiring "special education" provisions but also to those who need supplementary "life skills," vocational skills, remedial or additional language competencies.

— *cultural and religious traditions*: Many communities have not relinquished their assumed duty to provide learning that recognises their own traditions, even in the face of state resistance.

There are variations in the mix of inputs available for education: across countries and localities the inputs officially required for school education may not be available in the ratios and combinations or in the manner that may be desirable from a conventional perspective. These inputs concern:

— teaching staff with appropriate qualifications

— educational spaces

— resources for learning educational technologies.

Poor availability of one input may need to be compensated through increased attention to others, such as lower qualified staff by high-quality learning materials. The interpretations of the very inputs themselves may need to be adjusted, such as the "quality" of teaching staff or what constitute appropriate "educational spaces."

There is much learning ongoing outside the conventional school system that is not officially recognized and may not be captured in official data collection. This involves:

— childhood learning in homes and communities, including much locally relevant knowledge and skills. Although children enter schooling with this wealth of prior learning outcomes, it is generally not used as a basis for new learning.

— ongoing informal learning in social and work situations: The relevance of informal learning and its relationship with school learning has still not been sufficiently explored and captured in more comprehensive methods for assessing learning achievement.

— organised and structured forms of "non-formal" learning involving private and community-based provisions such as community schools, Koranic schools, open and distance learning arrangements, and traditional apprenticeships.

The "demand-side" of education, constituting individual learners, parents and communities, with their ever stronger interest in the value of learning, its quality and in notions of equity, can no longer be ignored. It tends to be particularly expressed in concerns regarding:

— the social and economic value of outcomes in respect to improving quality of life and access to work

— the quality of institutional provision for learning

— attention to home languages as well as access to languages of power and economy

— participation in learning as a lifelong possibility

— equity as regards personal and social costs of education.

There is a de facto wide diversity in the resourcing of education:

— The state does not have a monopoly of subsidization.

— Individuals and communities tend to be strongly interested in contributing towards what they regard as good education.

— There is an expanding interest of the private sector in playing a role: this tends to be reflected in physical facilities, in technological applications and learning resources, as well as in school-business linkages.

There is nothing new in recognising the important roles of different types of education, the insight required at the end of this century is that access to meaningful basic education for all can only be assured if there is wide recognition of the need for diversity in education provisioning. Given the continued relevance of social, economic, and political functions of education, such recognition of diversity is only possible in the context of maintaining essential parameters of a formal education system. Thus it has become necessary to argue for a transcendence of a de facto existence of separate systems and a move towards a unified but multi-form education system within which a variety of modalities for learning can exist side-by-side, but with visible equivalencies and identifiable linkages among them.

A system of "integrated diversity" might need to adopt several key characteristics. In pedagogical terms the system would follow an outcomes-based approach, whereby learning outcomes are defined in terms of a basic knowledge and skills profile allowing for locally adapted teaching and learning strategies and content. The common basic profile enables core achievement (not necessarily including all learning) to be assessed through standardised instruments leading to common certification. Within such overarching framework it would be acceptable to promote a differentiated set of provisions for learning, within which the conventional school will be probably be the main form but by no means the only one. A support infrastructure for administrative and professional services accessible to all provisions within the system. A funding framework that ensures acceptable equity in access to state subsidisation. An overall quality assurance system that enables diverse forms of provision to grow but within a frame of strict criteria for access and quality.

Within this context the conventional distinction between formal and non-formal education would become largely irrelevant. If the "formal" essentially refers to a provision operating within the above systems framework, then many "non-formal" arrangements could become formal while preserving, if not enhancing, their non-conventional features. "Non-formal," in this case only remains relevant in respect to learning arrangements that have mainly an intrinsic value and need not align themselves to the formal system's umbrella. Whereas provisions for learning could be different with respect to a variety of inputs, they would develop equity where it matters most: in the outcomes and future value of the learning acquired.

A re-examination of the experiences of traditionally non-formal education programmes is necessary in order to establish their contribution towards a wider systems framework for formal basic education. This agenda goes beyond investigations into the specific experiences and successes of individual programmes but attempts to come to grips with the potential of non-conventional approaches to education as regards improving access, quality, relevance, and cost-effectiveness of formal basic education across the system. In pursuing such an agenda a distinction needs to be made between non-formal education as a separate type of provision, on the one hand, and as an approach to learning or its provision in a generic sense, on the other hand. The former would examine the merits of specific adaptations for categories of learners with common socio-economic circumstances. The latter is likely to be much more challenging as it would seek to establish whether there are certain modalities of management, school-community linkages, or the organisation and methodology of the teaching-learning process that could have benefits across the system and allow all schools discretion to adjust to the needs and circumstances of their clienteles. This in turn could identify an agenda for a degree of deformalisation of schooling, or, within our new systems perspective, a degree of "loosening up the straitjacket."

Within the context of a system's agenda for promoting improvements in formal basic education, attention would have to go towards compensatory and alternative NFE provisions. Compensatory programmes intend to compensate young people for lack of access, eviction, or poor performance of the school system, while alternative programs aim to create an alternative to the mainstream provision, one that is meant to be more relevant and better suited to the basic learning needs of young people.

Recent literature on NFE provisions in terms of compensatory and alternative programmes confirms that the key principles that characterise this effort are flexibility and responsiveness to the needs of learners and their contexts. Thus community schools and related programmes have adjusted their timetables, their facilities, the provision of staff and materials to what makes sense under the circumstances, and they focus their curriculum on what appears to be the most pressing learning needs of their clienteles. In the process they forge close links with the surrounding communities and achieved a degree of community participation. At the same time we learn that NFE provisions have predominantly taken off in disadvantaged rural communities (and sometime peri-urban communities) and that the instigators tend to be external NGOs interested in the contribution of education to poverty alleviation. From a systemic perspective there are some questions which can be raised here:

— To what extent are the characteristics of flexibility and responsiveness mainly a response to efforts to provide formal education under conditions of poverty?

— To what extent have there been conscious efforts to implement adjustments in such way that they provide cost-effective alternatives towards promoting learning that is at least of equal standard to the level of the state schools?

— Have there been successful efforts to create learning situations, which address more effectively the needs of learners than tends to be the case in conventional schools?

— Has the responsiveness to demand produced learning outcomes that effectively assisted disadvantaged youngsters to progress in the education system or to enter the world of work?

— Has the involvement of communities evoked a type of ownership and influence that has distinct advantages for the learners as well as for the communities themselves?

— Is there an emergence of a methodology for sensitizing and preparing communities and ministries for assuming responsibilities for NFE programmes as part of a drive to expand and improve educational opportunities?

Although a fair bit of research into current seemingly successful programmes, such as community or village schools, has been ongoing, it seems still too early to provide conclusive answers to the above questions. However, some generalisable findings are emerging. For example, most community schools are clearly initiated in order to create additional school places in deprived areas for those children who for various reasons cannot attend formal schooling. As they mainly compensate for the inability of the state to expand access they tend to adopt features of conventional schools.

Core adjustments made to the conditions of poverty have a potential value of improving quality and effectiveness, though not necessarily at lower costs. Such adjustments include, for example, the utilization of less qualified and untrained teachers, the reduction of the curriculum to core subjects or their condensation into a fast-track option, and the adherence to smaller class sizes. There is evidence that this combination, with the add-ons of induction training, provision of basic materials, and regular supervision can produce satisfactory results in terms of both sustained participation and learning achievements. However, there is also evidence of problematic issues. These include the extent of the adaptation of the curriculum to the needs of learners in terms of background, age, and gender; the extent of introducing alternative teaching/learning strategies; and the ensuring of effective community ownership, in terms of participation in management and in curriculum implementation.

As regards efforts to adapt the curriculum and teaching/learning strategies the adjustments appear to take their cues more from the circumstances of learners than from their specific learning needs. Thus they tend to deal more with organisational arrangements than pedagogical content and styles. Gender issues have been accepted as a key concern, as higher female enrolment seems easier to achieve than an improvement in girls' performance. A particular vexing problem has been that NFE programmes tend to be introduced in poorer communities, with the result that the already disadvantaged end up contributing disproportionately to the cost of education. It is striking that the involvement of the donor tends to emphasize the provision of inputs that the state accepts as its normal responsibility but cannot provide. Thus the idea appears to be that community schools fill a void until the state can extend its accepted obligations.

Where the state does get involved, it effectively supports the emergence of an adapted form of the same conventional school system. Despite efforts at sensitisation, there is little indication as yet of attempts to promote a community perspective on the nature of basic education and its provision. This raises questions about the dynamics of community ownership and participation in a programme that appears to be compensatory and does not address the rules governing the provision of mainstream education themselves. If we return to the earlier expressed concerns regarding the development of a systemic framework that would cater more adequately for the kind of premises as outlined, one would particularly look for innovative work in areas like the following:

— teacher recruitment and professional support services

— curriculum: content and methods, and classroom practices

— language in education

— school / teacher supervision

— development and utilization of resource materials

— institutional decision-making and organisational culture

— community ownership, management, and participation

— improved cost-effectiveness.

Innovations in NFE in these areas could be appraised for their possible introduction into the mainstream of a formal basic education system and thus produce a wider impact of NFE as an approach to education. However, in spite of the many experiences, sometimes over long periods, there appears as yet to be little clarity about what can be replicated. Provisional evidence points to some elements that have significant consequences for access or quality. These include:

— a location for learning close to the home;

— the offering of reduced or condensed versions of a curriculum;

— the inclusion of home languages and local knowledge;

— community control over schools and teachers; the recruitment of local teachers, even if untrained;

— regular supervision of staff;

— small classes.

So far, however, none of these elements constitute new insights, and several are not peculiar to NFE programmes. The exceptions may be: the learning close to home, the reduced curriculum, and the recruitment of local teachers. In principle these three aspects do constitute an alternative provision, though they do not necessarily add up to a very different learning experience. Within a systems perspective there are specific elements of NFE that deserve further scrutiny. Those that have special relevance in linking NFE to the mainstream are:

— curriculum and assessment

— accreditation of teachers

— supervision by the ministry of education

— access to state funding.

These elements would ensure that the NFE provision is covered by the systemic umbrella as outlined earlier. They would also determine formal recognition as well as the right of transfer to other parts of the education system. Not in the least they are the basis for parity and viability, and thus address the basic issue of equity. In this respect there is still an absence of actual evidence: to what extent these links exist, how effective they are in reality, and what obstacles would need to be overcome.

The general agenda that the above approach entails can be seen foremost as a research and development one. It will inform further agendas related to advocacy and awareness as well as institutional reform and development. This R&D relates to the magnitude of the work to be done on desirable and effective learning outcomes in basic education.

This would reach beyond the core skills of literacy and numeracy, moving into knowledge of the social and ecological environment, life skills and a variety of competencies associated with science and technology, and arts and culture.

Further work would relate to forms of assessment that can effectively capture a wide variety of competencies and that are culturally sensitive. Probably the most critical work would be in the area of teaching and learning styles and in investigating the quality and effectiveness of different institutional and social arrangements for learning. It is in these fields that the implications of recognizing diversity of circumstances and needs would require the highest attention of academics, policy-makers, and practitioners combined.

Role of Technology in Non-formal Education

Technology, both of the high and law types has a very important role to play in assisting non-formal education The educator and the learner want to be successful in their educational activities. Methods that will assist in the process, then, are likely to be used, if known. Technology, provides some of these methods. The particular contribution of technology is that it assists learning by appealing to the human senses, sight, hearing and touch. As learning centrally involves a physiological process, it is argued that making an appeal to one or more of the senses increases the potential for learning or the speed of learning, or even the enjoyment or excitement of learning.

There are various means for classifying the various types of technology used as aids in the educational process. The main five categories and some examples of the technologies associated with each category are discussed below.

a) *Visual/non-project*: This category contains a large number of items. The aids rely on their visual impact without the aid of projection. A very important item in this category is the printed word: books, newspapers, journals, periodicals and newsletters, the favourite means for networks and NGOs.

   Newspapers are a 'forgotten medium for adult education'. Further, newspapers, either the large distribution dailies or cheaply made local news sheets, are a valuable and relevant reading resource for neo-literates. The category also includes a wide range of boards on which to write or draw illustrations such as the chalk or white board. There are newer types of this style of aid on which you can write in a marking pen and then have a single photocopy of the material written on the board. Then there are flipcharts, white paper held together and written upon and then either discarded or filpped over so that another sheet can be used. This first category includes photographs, photocopies and prints, charts, graphs or posters.

   Combinations of media can be used so that pictures can be placed on a felt board to help narrate a story or illustrate a problem. There is some scope with some of these items to involve the sense of touch. Participants can place the felt pictures on the board or they can be encouraged to handle the materials or re-locate parts of the village model in different places.

However, the emphasis is on the visual sense frequently as an aid to the spoken voice.

b) *Visual projected*: Items in this category include a range of what are commonly called 'transparencies'. These may be in the form of a long film called a strip film because it can be wound through the projector backwards and forwards to allow the learners to see the material on each frame of film. There are also slides, i.e. individual film transparencies.

There are normally projected one at a time but there are projectors that allow them to be shown rapidly one after the other because the individual slides are housed in a cartridge or carousel. The device called the overhead projector allows the instructor to present material prepared on thin sheets of transparent material to a group. The nature of the overhead projector is such that complex overheads can be prepared using overlays to illustrate complex ideas and systems.

A great deal of information can be miniaturised and stored in micro-film. A special micro-film reader enlarges the small print so that is easily read by the naked eye. Usually only one to three people can read such material at one time unless another form of projection is also used.

c) *Audio*: Items in this category include radio, vinyl records, tapes, the compact disc, language laboratories and the telephone. Radio can be thought of as a mass medium broadcasting to large numbers over vast distances. However, the development of small and efficient transmitters has resulted in radio becoming a much more localised medium so that local and regional communities can have access to the medium not only as listeners but as broadcasters and presenters. The nature of recordings has changed from the large and easily broken recordings of the 1940s to the compact disc of the 1980s. The large tape recorder of the 1950s has largely been replaced by small cassette players.

The storage of cassettes is also easier than reel tapes or even large vinyl recordings. The language laboratory consists of a number of tape recorder-type outlets set up in individual booths with headphones, and a central control panel as is demonstrated from the diagram.

The individual learner in the booth is able to follow the taped instruction, and sometimes provide oral feed-back, while the person at the central control can monitor the individual booths. The name language laboratory has been used because the item has been extensively used in the teaching of foreign languages. The telephone is not only a medium for one to one communication.

By using a telephone with an attached speaker-microphone one person can talk in a two-way discussion with a group. An extension of this is to have a group of people in scattered locations linked together through the telephone system so that they can communicate with each other. Such a process is called a teleconference. Not all telephone systems, particularly in developing nations, have the technical sophistication to carry the teleconference operation.

d) *Visual projected with audio*: This category include various sorts of movie film, television transmission, and video-recordings. Television in its transmitted form was well established in Western nations before the advent of video-recorder. In some developing countries the video-recorder has arrived in many locations before broadcast television. Efficient and comparatively cheap television transmitters may provide the opportunity, as with radio, of more locally produced and operated broadcast television.

An interesting combination of two items mentioned above illustrates this category. The tape-slide presentation combines the audio of the tape with the visual of the projected slide. Special techniques have been developed to make the automatic movement of the slides synchronise with the sounds of the tape recording. Items in this category are at the 'high tech' end of the spectrum of aids for teaching/learning.

Some of the refinements of the above items include closed-circuit television (CCTV) by which an educational program can be produced in one part of a building and shown in another part. It is television with limited transmission. Also, the item teleconferencing, noted in 3 above, can be conducted using visuals and voice and is called video-teleconferencing. Such a process is also called 'interactive' because those involved in the various locations can interact with one another.

The transmission of such video-teleconferencing has been facilitated, as has normal television and voice transmission, but the use of satellites. However, such techniques can also be carried out through terrestrial communication technology.

e) *Manual*: This category includes such devices as sewing machines and typewriters. And the recent items in this category are based on the 'key board'.

The micro-chip has resulted in the teaching machines becoming museum pieces. The computer has been used to develop a whole range of teaching programs. As the learner sits at the keyboard and manually operates the computer in performing tasks, the computer indicates the level of success, whether the learner can proceed to further instruction or whether remedial exercises have been diagnosed. Two frequently used terms in computer learner are computer assisted learning (CAL) and computer manager learning (CML).

So as to provide a balance and to avoid getting lost in high tech, it is important to note that there have been other 'touch' technological aids, for example blocks and marbles, and of course Cuisenaire rods. One of the oldest of these aids is the abacus, and there is its modern counterpart needing batteries the calculator. They have been significant developments linking the computer with satellites to educational institutions, other learners or resource centres. There are endless possibilities of linking various form of technological aids and methods.

These five categories provide a basis for gathering together the wide range of technological learning aids, the categories are not exclusive and combinations of methods from different categories may provide the required method for a specific purpose with a group of learners.

NFE planners and personnel need to be conscious of the cots of NFE programming. Note was also made of such approaches as cost-benefit and cost-effectiveness. The area of the use of technology to support learning is a very useful area to apply these principles because on the one hand some technology is very expensive and on the other there is continuing question of the choice between a range of alternatives. What are the comparative costs, for example, of developing a set of videos or a set of photographs or board figures for a felt board to support a nutrition-improvement program? Then other questions, as to how many need to be produced, how will they be distributed and at what cost, what will be the costs of substitute or replacement materials and will there be location costs involved in their use, will require costing. These can be calculated. Then the assumptions have to be made about how many people can be reached with the various methods being investigated and the final, the really difficult question, to be answered on the basis, preferably of evaluations of previous uses of the methods, is how effective the various methods are likely to be.

Then the costs are related to effectiveness and a decision made on which method. This can appear a simple approach. There are, however, difficulties. There frequently significant indirect costs. They may include hidden 'subsidies' such as the cost of transport or of studio time or of the un-charged for work time of staff. In areas of technology, there are also what is known as 'infra-structure' costs, for example making certain that the telephone system can carry the required teleconference calls or that there is sufficient power for projector generation.

The cultural implications of the use of technology as an aid to learning in NFE need to be carefully considered. It is not adequate to apply the sorts of 'best use', 'advantages/disadvantages' approaches developed in Western nations to other cultural settings. There is also the question of 'technology transfer', that is taking some piece of technology, developed in one culture, and using it in another. The agricultural system was referred to in the introduction. In this context, the notion of technology transfer may refer to the introduction of tractors developed for Western agriculture into the farming systems of Africa or Asia.

Importance of learning in the use of technology has resulted in modifications being sometimes made to the technology. For example, because movie films are often long and do not provide the opportunity for those watching to talk about the content of the movie, there developed trigger films. There were short films that posed an issue, usually dramatically. Then the film was stopped and the audience discussed the issue in groups, frequently suggesting 'what would happen next'. Then the film was re-commenced and 'a' particular solution or version of what might happen was played out on the screen and after the movie was complete the audience were able to discuss the movie interpretation in relation to the scenarios they had developed. Having a clear priority for the sorts of activities in which the learners will be involved results usually in a variety of technology being used. There is a danger in the use of technology in learning that the learners may be just entertained or that so much technology is provided that there is no active learning planned for the learners.

Having the equipment is one area of concern, having people who can work the equipment, and attend to breakdowns, is another question, frequently overlooked. These technology-literate people may not be part of the NFE system, but from wherever they are obtained, they need to be present and at the ready.As far as the NFE staff are concerned, there is needed to be technology literate. But what that really means is unclear as the more general question of what general literacy means. They should know how to operate and make running repairs to the equipment. Such knowledge is not gained in a one-off learning experience. Technology changes. If personnel are to be given a full or partial responsibility in relation to technology, it is vital that opportunities be given for them to upgrade their knowledge and skills and the technology, particularly if it is high tech, becomes more sophisticated. If technological specialists are employed, then it should be expected that their knowledge, as with all specialists, will, or should, become sop specialised that the other non-specialists in the organisation will not understand what they are understanding.

8

Strategic Approach to Educational For All

The World Education Forum held in Dakar, Senegal, 26-28 April 2000, adopted the Dakar Framework for Action which contains overall goals and commitments of governments and the international community for achieving basic education for all by 2015. The goals aim at ensuring, in particular, quality primary education for all and gender equality for all levels of education by 2015, appropriate education for all out-of-school young people and under-educated adults, and recognized and measurable learning outcomes at all levels and for all educational activities.

Education For All (EFA) goals adopted by the world education forum, Dakar, April 2000, include:

(i) expanding and improving comprehensive early childhood care and education, especially for the most vulnerable and disadvantaged children;

(ii) ensuring that by 2015 all children, particularly girls, children in difficult circumstances and those belonging to ethnic minorities, have access to and complete free and compulsory primary education of good quality;

(iii) ensuring that the learning needs of all young people and adults are met through equitable access to appropriate learning and life skills programmes;

(iv) achieving a 50 per cent improvement in levels of adult literacy by 2015, especially for women, and equitable access to basic and continuing education for all adults;

(v) eliminating gender disparities in primary and secondary education by 2005, and achieving gender equality in education by 2015, with a focus on ensuring girls' full and equal access to and achievement in basic education of good quality;

(vi) improving all aspects of the quality of education and ensuring excellence of all so that recognized and measurable learning outcomes are achieved by all, especially in litera cy, numeracy and essential life skills.

If EFA goals are to be attained they must first be translated into national EFA plans and action programmes. Without realistic plans and programmes, countries and the international donor community have little chance of ever seeing these goals attained. National EFA plans are the sine qua non condition for effectively reaching the EFA goals.

Levels of Educational Planning

The overriding goal of educational activities is to serve the needs of children in the context of their national, cultural, ethnic, religious, social and economic environments. Consequently, the ultimate aim of the planning process concerned with formal basic education is to serve the needs of children of school age at the level of the school or alternative programme. Therefore, the school level, cluster school level, or community level, can be called Planning Level-I. In order to function, schools need support from higher levels, such as townships, districts, provinces, etc., which is Planning Level-II. These entities, in turn, need guidance and support from the central, national level, which is Planning Level-III.

All three levels have to work together; but each level has specific functions and tasks. Although different systems exist in countries in Asia, the most common structure appears to be the following.

Planning Level-I is concerned with matters such as organising the teaching/learning process and parent and community participation.

Planning Level-II is concerned with support, such as teacher training, provision of teaching and learning materials, personnel management, major construction and maintenance to ensure access to education, some resource allocation, efficiency of resource utilisation, and mobilising of funding.

Concerns of Planning Level-III include ensuring national standards for, and unity of, curriculum, textbooks, exams, teacher training, personnel management, resource allocation to ensure access to quality education, resource utilisation, ensuring donor relations, and sector reform and development.

In a growing number of countries the planning functions and tasks of these levels are in a process of change. For example, decentralization is moving many tasks to lower levels, including tasks like teacher training, personnel management, fund-raising, and infrastructure management.

The planning concept to be applied in each country will have to be based on a matrix which shows what level is presently responsible for which functions and tasks and then plan for the changes which should occur in this matrix over time.

These three levels are directly involved in short term planning, particularly the annual budgeting process. Medium-term planning requires the involvement of Levels II and III. Long-term planning is usually primarily the concern of Level-III. Drawing up the EFA plan 2002-2015 is a joint task of Levels II and III. Through appropriate participatory mechanisms and process, Level I (the level of schools and school clusters) is also involved in planning, particularly in EFA planning. The active participation of Level-I is essential when, once the EFA plan has been adopted, implementation action plans are being prepared.

Planning proceeds in three successive stages; each stage corresponds to a particular type of plan: first long-term planning (plan covering ten years or more), then medium-term planning (plan covering three to five years), and finally short-term planning (plan linked to the government budget cycle).

Today, most countries already have a long-term education plan (in a variety of forms: as part of the national development plan, or as a master plan for the different education sub-sectors, or as general education sector plan), which sets the long-term policy goals. By nature, long-term plans are quite general.

Much more detailed concepts are needed for making resource allocation decisions and for making sure that enough financial, material and human resources are available to carry out activities required to attain the long-term goals. Therefore, many countries are now concentrating their planning efforts on the design of medium-term plans, since they are closer, in terms of both time horizon and detail of content, to resource allocation cycles.

The national EFA plan to be prepared for the period 2002-2015 will have typical features of both long-term and medium-term plans. On the one hand, the EFA plan will set overall, long term policy goals to be reached by the year 2015; on the other hand, it will also set specific medium-term targets and priorities, and outline implementation programmes for concrete action for the first five or six years of the plan period.

— *Stage 1:* Preparing the long-term plan: By setting overall policy goals, the long-term plan determines the general, basic concepts and principles for education compatible with each country's intrinsic values, its current needs and future expectations. It outlines the overall resource requirements for the sector in the long run. It is the outcome of political decisions taken in the context of the overall social and economic development policies of the country.

— *Stage 2:* Preparing the medium-term plan: The medium term plan defines what needs to be done, when, how and with what resource inputs, in order to attain the long-term policy goals. It sets specific objectives and targets and outlines implementation programmes and implementation modalities. It contains a finance plan, identifying national as well as external sources of funding.

— *Stage 3:* Preparing a short-term plan (also called implementation plan): Implementation plans lay out the details of what will be done, by whom, how, with what amount of resources and financed by what sourc e s. Usually spanning a period of a few budget years, they are broken down by annual budgets, setting the specific targets to be attained in the context of the fiscal or budget year.

In most countries, education planning focuses on a number of key concerns, around which education plans are structured, including:

— access to schooling, i.e. access to the first grade of the primary and secondary education cycle, and the possibility to complete the full cycle; access to alternative approaches to providing basic education (for those children who have no access to formal basic education); including key factors such as classrooms, teachers, teaching/learning materials, language, an enabling social and physical environment; access to education for girls, and other excluded groups;

— quality of the teaching/learning process, content, structure of the system, learning achievements, and relevance of the curriculum to cultural, social and economic goals of national development;

— sector m a n a g e m e n t, including the regulatory framework, resource allocation, resource utilization, policy setting and planning, implementation monitoring and evaluation of results, and decentralization.

Preparing an education plan is a process aimed at identifying the most appropriate course of action to address issues, set priority objectives and targets, and provides the basis for cost-effective resource allocation. The plan preparation process consists of a sequence of four phases, including:

— *Phase-1*: finding the facts about how the sector functions today and identifying issues that need to be addressed in the future, as well as strengths that need to be maintained or reinforced in the future, and undertaking a sector analysis or a more limited situation analysis;

— *Phase-2*: charting the future, i.e. preparing the plan, by setting policy goals and strategic objectives, formulating implementation programmes, setting targets, assessing resource requirements, setting priorities and designing implementation strategies;

— *Phase-3:* designing the action by drawing up outline implementation plans. This step has in recent years begun to be included in the planning process, particularly in the preparation of medium term plans. Drawing up detailed action plans is not part of preparing long term or medium term plans. Detailed action or implementation plans are drawn up once the medium-term plan has been approved by the government and the relevant legislative bodies, and correspond to the first step of implementation of the medium term plan.

— *Phase-4:* adopting the plan as an official government document with normative status, orienting laws, statutory decisions, and budgets. The planning process includes monitoring of the plan implementation, regular updating of sector analysis information, assessing the results and impact of implementation and feeding back this information into adjustments of policies and implementation strategies throughout the period of plan implementation.

— *Phase-5*: implementing and monitoring the plan implementation. The monitoring information is fed back into the plan implementation process and used to review the plan regularly and adapt it as necessary to changing needs and conditions within the overall planning framework.

— *Phase-6*: evaluating the plan, including its achievements in terms of reaching stated qualitative and quantitative objectives and targets, producing expected outcomes and impact on priority target groups, as well as its cost-effectiveness. The results of the evaluation are used to improve the planning and policy setting process in consecutive plans.

Depending on what type of plan is being prepared the planning process

— puts emphasis on different aspects,

— involves specific partners and stakeholders as active participants in the preparation of the plan, and

— uses specific approaches.

The planning process generates information and provides an overview of the present situation of the education and training system against which it will be possible to monitor plan implementation and assess performance and impact of programmes and activities. This will permit identifying needs, revising implementation programmes, and then, designing measures to adjust plan implementation as and when needed, and not only when the next plan is drawn up in five or ten years time.

Education sector analysis

Education sector analysis is a comprehensive analysis of the current situation and functioning of the education and training sector, or of a sub-sector, and therefore the necessary first phase in the planning process. Without being based on sector analysis information, the plan runs the risk of not being sufficiently rooted in reality and establishing unrealistic targets and actions.

Sector analysis consists in the collecting and analysing of basic data which yield necessary insight into the functioning of the educational system, making it possible to diagnose causes of malfunctioning, underachievement and inefficient utilization of resource. It identifies and helps to understand the major shortcomings, and formulates realistic assumptions about the cause and effect relations that condition the performance of the educational system. Sector analysis also includes the identification of possible responses to the problems.

A typical sector analysis collects information and conducts analysis on major areas and their components:

— *Performance of the sector (sub-sector)*: access (admission, transition rates, enrolment rates), enrolment (by gender, geographical area, home language), internal efficiency, learning conditions (pupils-class ratio, pupil-teacher ratio), learning achievement, teaching staff , physical facilities, teaching/learning materials, curriculum, teaching methodology, examinations and certification, relevance to manpower needs of the economy, costs, financing; contextual aspects such as the community served by the school, and social and economic factors which impact on the educational system in terms of access to and demand for educational services. Among social factors are, for example, the social characteristics of the learners, the learning environment and the environment in which the teacher works.

— *Management of the education system:* management of pedagogical services, including teacher training, teacher support services (inspection, resource centres), curriculum and teaching/learning material development; administrative and financial management, including personnel (recruitment, career, salary), budget and expenditure, efficiency of resource utilization, community participation.

— *Policy management:* planning and budgeting, resource allocation, costs of access to education, monitoring, evaluation of impact, donor coordination.

The areas covered by sector analysis may be defined in other ways, such as grouping the components according to criteria which are appropriate for the sector policy environment of the country concerned. A structure often used is: access to education, quality and relevance of education, and sector management.

Undertaking sector analysis results in a number of important side effects that contribute to improving the management of the education system. One is the discovery of weaknesses in data collection, data management and analysis, and in dissemination and use of basic data and analytical information.

In a growing number of countries, sector analysis is instrumental in identifying the causes of conceptual inadequacies and of non-performance of educational management information systems (EMIS). Responding to these findings through quick action can improve the data system, thus strengthening the basis for monitoring of plan implementation and evaluation. Another important side effect is the cooperation generated by sector analysis:

(a) among the providers of analytical information which are compelled, by the rigor of sector analysis, to compare and align methodologies, definitions, coverage, explanations and analysis, and

(b) between the providers and the users of analytical information whereby the providers are induced to revise their ways of working and start providing information which is effectively needed by the users, and whereby the users are compelled to understand and use analytical information as an essential input into their decision making.

These side effects of sector analysis are significant and very effective contributions to improving the quality and relevance of the planning process.

A complete sector analysis includes surveys and studies aimed at filling information gaps and providing insights into the complex relationships between resource inputs and teaching/learning outcomes, and on factors which determine private demand for education.

There is no standardized way of presenting sector analysis information. In some countries it has been more detailed and rigorous than in others, depending on the availability of reliable data and on the time and resources available to undertake the work. If the time and the resources available to prepare the plan are not enough for a complete sector analysis to be carried out, sector analysis can be undertaken as a synthesis of existing data and other relevant information. In most countries, a large amount of information already exists that can be used, thus saving time and allowing sector analysts to move into plan preparation more quickly.

Sector information is generally available in papers, reports, working documents, studies, and surveys generated by donor-funded activities. Bringing all this information together into a sector analysis is a difficult task requiring high professional skills. Yet, without it, the planning process would be truncated, and the plan would have no roots. Sector analysis is the starting point for all types of long term and medium term planning.

Undertaking sector analysis is both an informative and a formative process. It creates awareness and understanding on the part of the stakeholders associated to the work, thereby laying the ground for a realistic dialogue later on during the plan preparation process, particularly when objectives and targets are being set. To achieve this, sector analysis must be carried out in a participatory way, involving principal actors, including public authorities, NGOs, organizations and associations of civil society (CSO), and in some countries, religious leaders. It must take into account the results of studies and ongoing analysis undertaken by donors and in the framework of wider international programmes, for example, the United Nations Development Assistance Framework (UNDAF).

Plan Preparation Steps

Once sector analysis is completed and has provided the necessary base information the preparation of the plan can begin. There is no standard approach for preparing the plan. A widely applied approach to preparing long-term and, particularly, medium-term plans, which has proven to be relatively simple, efficient and adaptable to specific country situations, consists of the following principle plan preparation steps:

— *Step-1:*

(a) identifying the goals and objectives adopted by the government for the plan period;

(b) identifying possible responses and solutions to the issues and problems which have been identified by the sector analysis; responses and solutions being expressed as objectives and as outline programmes (with outlines of activities and measures) to be undertaken in order to reach the targets and objectives;

(c) setting preliminary targets for each programme (and the activities needed to reach the targets);

— *Step-2:* assessing the resource implications of the proposed responses and solutions; by projecting the development of each cost-creating component of the education system and estimating the total. The principal components include: pupil enrolment, teachers, physical facilities, teaching/learning materials, activities aimed at ensuring access to and quality and relevance of education, and sector management.

— *Step-3*: assessing the feasibility and affordability of the proposed solutions; by

(3.1) estimating the likely availability of funds (share of education in government budget; distribution of these funds within the education sector, i.e. between the different sub-sectors; cost-sharing possibilities);

(3.2) estimating the likely availability of non-financial inputs such as teachers, premises, textbooks, which depend on the respective production capacity, as well as funding;

(3.3) assessing the organizational and management capacity likely to be available to ensure the normal functioning of the education system and to carry out reform and development activities; and

(3.4) identifying likely resource gaps;

— *Step-4*: designing alternative strategies to reach the objectives and targets;

(4.1) identifying measures to close the resource gap, such as:(a) reducing the costs of the education system by improving the cost-efficiency of resource utilization (which includes changing of targets and of technical coefficients which determine the way in which the sector functions; (b) mobilizing additional resources; (c) encouraging the creation of private education institutions; and (d) lobbying by the education authorities for a higher share of the national budget for the education sector;

(4.2) revising some of the proposed programmes and activities; and

(4.3) agreeing on the final EFA targets and priorities.

— *Step-5*: formulating the plan by deciding on definite objectives, targets, programmes, activities, priorities, resources needed, financing, and implementation scheduling.

— *Step-6*: preparing implementation action plans: In order to increase (a) the chances of obtaining consensus among the principal stakeholders concerning the proposed plan, and (b) the chances of obtaining the required funding for plan implementation, in a growing number of countries, Ministries of Education include in the medium-term education plan more or less detailed action programmes (or action plans, or implementation action plans). This is a way to respond effectively to the principal concerns and expectations of stakeholder groups. In these cases, preparing implementation action plans is included in the planning process (Step-6).

Plan preparation steps-1, -2 and -3 are technical in nature and involve experts (analysts, educators, planners, researchers, statisticians, etc.). They are carried out through fact finding, desk work, workshops, involving consultations with, and participation by local communities, schools, teachers, NGOs and other actors. By contrast, Plan preparation step-4 is the central policy part of planning. During this step stakeholders exercise their influence to promote specific concepts, objectives and targets to be considered in policy formation. In a modern planning process this step is often organized to a very large extent in the form of dialogue between the stakeholders, bringing them together in seminars, roundtable meetings and other appropriate forms of consultation aimed at (i) providing the planners with the opportunity to reflect the interests and needs of stakeholder groups in the formulation of targets, proposed programmes and modalities for implementation as realistic as possible, and (ii) building consensus for the objectives and programmes of the plan, thereby strengthening the chances of enlisting their support for plan implementation.

Plan preparation step-4 is also the step where the issue of sustainability has to be carefully assessed. In order to succeed, education initiatives have to be sustained politically and financially, as well as socially and culturally, over long periods of time. The long-term implications of pursuing certain education policy options rather than others must be carefully weighed, against the outlook for (i) economic development, in particular, trained manpower requirements and public sector potential for financing education investments and recurrent expenditure, and (ii) social, cultural and political transformation.

The programmes and targets of the education plan are part of the overall national development efforts for the economy and society as a whole. They should be linked to existing socio-economic development plans and programmes, in particular national strategies related to poverty reduction, health service provision or other fields which affect the attainment of education development objectives.

For the allocation of financial resources the education plan competes with all the other sectors. Planners have to be careful to propose programmes which are set within reasonable limits of resource requirements and have a good chance of being funded and implemented. To do this requires overcoming two difficulties: (i) to decide at what stage in the planning process the resource-limitation aspects should be taken into account, and (ii) to obtain reliable indications of likely available resource levels.

Taking the resource limitation aspects into account is a consideration, which pervades and underlies the entire plan preparation process. Throughout plan preparation the planners must take into account the fact that other sub-sectors will also want the resources which the education sector is counting on. The usual way of making planning assumptions on resource ceilings for the education sector is to assume that the minimum ceiling in the future is the present share of the education sector in the national budget. However, in a situation where the education policy goals for the plan period imply an increase of the education sector share, the planners must seek to convince the providers of resources to change the resource allocation pattern in favour of education.

The planners can do this by closely associating the policy level of the Ministry of Education as well as the Ministry of Planning and the Ministry of Finance to the plan preparation work right from the start of the plan preparation process. In this way there is a good chance that the decision levels in the Planning and Finance Ministries will gain sufficient insight into the functioning of the education sector and a better understanding of the programmes included in the education plan, as (4.1) well as of the reasonableness of the resource requirements of the education sector.

Importance of National EFA Plans

The Dakar Framework for Action contains two fundamental conditions which must be fulfilled at the national level before partners in the international community will be prepared to contribute resources required for the implementation of the national EFA plan (The Dakar Framework for Action, para. 16 and 17):

— Condition-1 is that specific national processes for EFA development (and for the education sector as a whole) must be in place and functioning, including among others, government leadership, systematic consultation with national civil society, preparation and implementation of reforms addressing the EFA goals, a sustainable national funding framework, and coherence and synergy of all human development activities within the national development planning framework.

— Condition-2 is that a credible EFA plan must be in place.

The Dakar Framework for Action is a policy document reflecting the views of a large range of countries, regions, donors, technical assistance agencies and NGOs. It therefore contains little in the way of technical advice in drawing up national EFA plans. This EFA Planning Guide provides a technical concept that attempts to put the Dakar follow-up in the context of national plan preparation structures and mechanisms and makes sense professionally.

Principles guiding the preparation of national EFA plans have been defined in the Dakar Framework for Action.

Each National EFA Plan will:

(i) be developed by government leadership in direct and systematic consultation with national civil society;

(ii) attract co-ordinated support of all development partners;

(iii) specify reforms addressing the six EFA goals;

(iv) establish a sustainable financial framework;

(v) be time-bound and action oriented;

(vi) include mid-term performance indicators; and

(vii) achieve a synergy of all human development efforts, through its inclusion within the national development planning framework and process.

The EFA goals, their implied targets, and the guiding principles for national EFA plans have to be translated into operational, practical planning concepts. The Planning Guide attempts to do this within the technical framework of a professionally sound plan preparation approach.

The EFA plan is a long-term macro-plan, covering the 14-year period 2002-2015. It may be broken down into two medium-term phases, in line with specific national planning cycles. The plan for the first medium-term phase will be more detailed than the plan for the second medium-term phase. At the end of the first phase a mid-term review of plan implementation should be undertaken.

The EFA plan will be implemented through annual budgets which are integral parts of the national education budgets and, thus, the annual public sector budgets.

The EFA plan should not be an additional plan to already existing plans. Instead, the EFA plan should be a framework, in the form of a large programme, integrating in a coherent way all EFA aspects of all other presently valid plans and policy documents.

The EFA plan will be drawn up in a situation where other plans and programmes already exist which cover EFA aspects or are in other ways directly relevant to

EFA; such as the national development plan, the education sector plan, education sub-sector plans, other policy documents and strategic instruments (e.g. development concepts and strategies relevant to the education sector formulated by donors in partnership with EFA actors .

The coverage of EFA goes beyond the formal education system. It concerns a number of other government entities that carry out educational activities aimed at EFA target groups.

The ongoing and pipeline projects relevant to EFA of these other government bodies must also be taken into account in drawing up the EFA plan. Moreover, there are ongoing and planned donor financed projects which, in their totality, or with certain components, are directly relevant to EFA, although they may not have been developed within a national EFA concept. The EFA plan must also take them into account.

Once the EFA plan has integrated all EFA activities for the plan period into a coherent, sector-wide framework, all EFA activities foreseen for the EFA plan period, it guides the EFA activities of all government bodies. In fact, the normative function of this integrated EFA plan obliges all government bodies, as well as their external funding partners, to adhere to it and abstain from launching separate initiatives.

EFA plan: target groups

The EFA plan has four main target groups and three target sub-sectors. The are decribed in table 1. In most countries the priority EFA target is to provide access to formal education for as many children as possible and to reach universal primary (or universal lower secondary) education as soon as possible. Therefore, the principle EFA planning efforts in these countries concern formal basic education.

Table 1 EFA: Target groups

Target Group	*Corresponding Sub-sector*
(1) the young child from age 0 to 6 including infants and children in preschool age	Early childhood care and development (E C C D) and preschool
(2) children in formal basic education (with particular attention to girls) Subgroup (2.1): pupils who are already in the formal education system; Subgroup (2.2): children who are expected to enter grade-1 (i.e. primary education) and grade-7 (i.e. lower secondary education), and total enrolment in all grades	Formal basic education (for EFA purposes this comprises in most countries primary education, and in some countries also lower secondary education)
(3) out of school youth in the EFA-age range (with particular attention to girls) Subgroup (3.1): children who never enrolled, i.e. who never entered grade-1 (typically children in educationally under-served areas, minority groups, etc.) and grade-6 (primary education) leavers who do not enter grade-7 (lower secondary education); Subgroup (3.2): children who enter grade 1 and children who enter grade-7 but drop out before attaining the end of the cycle.	Non-formal education (NFE) and continuing education
(4) Adults below literacy level	Non-formal education (NFE) and continuing education

The ultimate EFA goal is to ensure full and quality education to all children in the primary age range and provide extended learning opportunities, in the form of formal basic education or non-formal equivalency programmes, for youth and adults. To attain this ultimate goal in the long term requires optimal resource allocation across sub-sectors; what is considered optimal will differ among countries and change as the system develops. In countries where financial resources are very limited, assigning priority of resource allocation to target groups, 1, 3 and 4 may appear to leave formal education underprovided, limiting its growth and improvement, which would result in more young people not having access to formal basic education or to drop out, thereby increasing the number of out-of-school children and youth and the EFA programmes and resources required for them. This may end up defeating the ultimate goal of EFA.

Phases and Steps of EFA Plan

A typical EFA plan might contain four sub-plans (one for each of the four target-groups) and a consolidated plan which brings together the four sub-plans into a coherent framework. Preparing the EFA sub-plans includes all essential phases and steps of education planning.

- *Phase-1*: situation analysis or sector analysis: finding out how the EFA sector (i.e. the various programmes and activities carried out in the country that are related to EFA) works at present, identifying the issues and possible responses;
- *Phase-2*: mapping the future course of EFA, i.e. identifying possible solutions to the issues (in the

form of programmes); setting preliminary targets and outlining activities needed to reach the targets; assessing the resources required; identifying likely resource gaps; identifying possibilities of reducing the resource gaps through improving the functioning of EFA and through mobilizing additional resources; setting the definite EFA targets and formulating the plan;

— *Phase-3*: preparing future action, by outlining implementation action plans, including among others, financing plans.

Target setting Process

The target setting process has two closely interrelated dimensions: a technical dimension, consisting of a sequence of rather complex tasks (as listed below); and a sector policy dimension, in the form of a dialogue and negotiation process among the principal stakeholders, under government leadership. Target setting for EFA is made particularly difficult by already existing plans and by ongoing and proposed donor projects which have components directly relevant to EFA.

Target setting involves a number of complex tasks:

(1) drawing up a complete overview of all components (programmes, activities, targets) contained in the already existing plans and projects and in pipeline projects relevant to EFA;

(2) formulating the programmes to be carried out in order to attain the EFA goals (e.g. a programme for improving the teaching-learning process in order to increase internal efficiency, learning outcomes and

access, which together help attaining EFA goals (ii), (iii) and (vi));

(3) dentifying the activities required in order to carry out the programmes (e.g. carrying out in-service teacher training, creating resource centres, revising teaching methodology, revising pre-service teacher training, strengthening advisory services to schools);

(4) defining the targets (e.g. number of teachers to be trained every year, number of resource centres to be set up);

(5) assessing the resources required (teachers, classrooms, teaching/learning materials, funding, management) to undertake the activities necessary in order to achieve the targets;

(6) assessing the feasibility and affordability of the activities and, thus, the targets; i.e. the task of identifying likely resource gaps, and

(7) in the inevitable case of foreseeable resource gaps, ensuring that the dialogue process among stakeholders aimed at identifying and agreeing on reasonable, realistic EFA targets and corresponding activities.

Since the already existing plans, and their ongoing implementation, may not plan ahead as far as 2015, the targets for the EFA plan must take into account:

(i) the targets in the existing plans, and

(ii) the results of the sector analysis which yield information on the progress achieved and problems that have arisen in reaching the targets.

The EFA plan has to be an integrated EFA programme (targets and activities) combining already existing plans, strategic instruments, and ongoing projects, makes it necessary to undertake a special kind of analysis: one which will establish consistency and compatibility between the targets, activities and resource requirements of the different EFA relevant parts of these plans and projects. This requires understanding of the different assumptions and methodologies used for preparing these plans and strategic instruments

Plan preparation process

The EFA plan is both a policy document, which reflects consensus among the stakeholders on goals, objectives, targets, and commitment to effectively provide the resources and the management support needed to attain them; and a technical document, containing the concrete, formal and accountable basis for sustainable action. It is this technical nature of the EFA plan which informs the policy consensus. It helps to minimize inappropriate decisions concerning programme content and resource allocation which are contrary to the plan and might jeopardize its efficient implementation.

All important national stakeholders must be associated at an appropriate stage of plan preparation. Participatory planning as referred to in the Dakar Framework for Action requires the involvement of a wide range of stakeholder groups from government institutions at all levels of the system, civil society and external donors. The ways in which this participatory process is being organized depend on the country's political traditions and existing legislative and institutional framework.

In many countries central institutions and technocratic approaches still prevail in the planning process. In those countries the Ministry of Education, as a first step, should associate other relevant government institutions and stakeholder groups organized at central level to the preparation of an outline EFA plan.

The outline plan should be drawn up in linkage with existing plans prepared by those institutions and results from previous consultations, and then become the basis for a wide dialogue among stakeholders. An inter-institutional central planning framework during the plan implementation will legitimize and support cross-sectoral local initiatives, which in the longer term will reinforce the momentum towards joint planning and wider stakeholder participation when follow-up plans are prepared.

Other approaches might be more appropriate in particular in countries with decentralized education management systems, where detailed EFA plans are needed at planning Level-II, and for those sub-sectors, in particular ECCD and NFE, that depend largely on funding and service provision from non-public sources. In those countries, and for those sub-sectors, all important national stakeholders should be associated to the plan preparation from the start, including representatives from civil society, NGOs and external donors.

It is also useful for major donors and technical assistance partners to be associated in the plan preparation process, since they will be instrumental in plan preparation. Associating them in some ways is particularly important at the point when programmes are being designed, targets and priorities set, and financing plans outlined. Close association of at least the principle donors to the plan preparation process will set the ground for close donor-government cooperation within the framework of a Sector Wide Approach (SWAp).

Because of the short time available, and also in order to ensure coherence between the different components of the EFA plan, plan preparation requires rigorous organization. A choice has to be made between different organizational approaches. For example, the following may appear to be feasible, particularly in view of the short time available to complete national EFA plans:

(i) plan preparation for the four target groups carried out by one planning group, composed of technical experts from different fields (planning, teacher training, curriculum development, language teaching, finance, management, non-formal education, preschool education, adult education, formal basic education); or

(ii) plan preparation entrusted to different groups (one for each of the four target groups, which could form sub-groups for specific areas such as curriculum, teacher training, finance, quality, etc.) which would be coordinated by a technical steering group which, in turn, reports to the National EFA Committee and works under its guidance.

The choice depends on the availability of national experts and on how the preparation of the plan is organized by the Government: as a professional, technical process, or as a participatory, consultative process, or a combination of both.

EFA programmes and educational development

EFA programmes are only a part of all education activities undertaken by the education system. They are, in fact, a sub-sector of the education sector, along with the sub-sectors of (upper) secondary education, vocational education, and higher education.

The EFA sub-sector is funded from the same sources as the other sub-sectors and it draws on the same kind of resources. It is competing for limited resources with the other sub-sectors. Therefore, the EFA plan has to be drawn up within reasonable resource limits, respecting a balance within the overall education sector. This balance is a political decision, taken at the level of the Minister of Education, who decides in close consultation with the Minister of Planning and the Minister of Finance.

Unless these Ministers agree, the EFA plan cannot be implemented. Harmonizing the EFA plan with the development plans of the other education sub-sectors is a consideration that pervades and underlies the entire planning Phase 2, i.e. the phase that charts the future. In each of the Plan Preparation Steps the planners must take into account the fact that other sub-sectors will also want the resources that EFA is counting on.

The planners can do this in several ways:

(i) by checking, at each plan preparation step, with the policy level of the Ministry of Education, as well as with the Ministry of Planning and the Ministry of Finance, whether the order of magnitude of resources, particularly financial resources, which they have in mind stands a reasonable chance of being accepted; or

(ii) by closely associating the policy level of the Ministry of Education as well as the Ministry of Planning and the Ministry of Finance in the plan preparation work, for example by including them in working groups.

The plan preparation steps which are crucial for gauging the future resource situation are Step-2 (assessment of the resources required), Step-3 (assessment of the likely availability of resources and identification of resource gaps) and Step-4 (identification of measures to close the resource gaps, including, among others, obtaining additional resources). Underlying these steps is a continuous, iterative process of putting forward programme proposals and related resource requirements and of revising them in the light of considerations and facts brought forward by the providers of resources.

Structure for an EFA plan

There is no standard structure for an EFA plan. The EFA plan document should be organized in a way that shows, for each of the four EFA target groups and for the corresponding sub-sectors, the situation analysis, the goals, the programmes, the activities and targets, the resource requirements and the terms of implementation management. The programmes could be presented in three broad groups which reflect the principle policy thrust: (i) access, (ii) quality and relevance, (iii) management. The plan must also show what is foreseen for specific target groups (girls, ethnic minorities, etc.) and situations (poverty, gender inequality, etc.).

EFA planning for non-formal Education

ECCD and non-formal and continuing education are an integral part of the enlarged vision of Education for All. The Dakar Framework for Action sets the following goals:

Table 2: non-formal Education: goals of Dakar Framework for Action

Dakar Framework for Action Goal	Target-group concerned		
	Group 1	Group 2	Group 4
Goal (i) expanding and improving comprehensive early childhood care and education, especially for the most vulnerable and disadvantaged children	X		
Goal (iii) ensuring that the learning needs of all young people and adults are met through equitable access to appropriate learning and life-skills programmes		X	X
Goal (iv) achieving a 50 per cent improvement in levels of adult literacy by 2015, especially for women, and equitable access to basic and continuing education for all adults			X
Goal (vi) improving all aspects of the quality of education and ensuring excellence of all so that recognized and measurable learning outcomes are achieved by all, especially in literacy, numeracy and essential life skills	X	X	X

The government has a smaller direct role in providing these three target groups with education (except for those children of school age who have never been to school or have dropped out. In most countries, the government is not obliged, neither by constitution nor an education law, to provide these target groups with free education. The government is, however, obliged to take every possible measure to help provide educational services to these groups. Such measures include the creation of the regulatory framework (policy, laws, rules, regulations) needed to encourage and facilitate NFE activities by other bodies, primarily civil society, employers and local communities. They include, in particular, rules concerning licensing, accreditation and operation of NFE activities, granting financial and material incentive, assisting with curriculum development and training of instructors, ensuring recognition of certificates and equivalency of non-formal and continuing education programmes with formal education validation.

The government may also act as partner to non-public NFE service providers by participating in joint NFE activities. The government's role includes also the setting of standards for quality and relevance (content, examinations and controlling their application) to ensure high learning achievement and nation-wide coherence of the education system.

EFA activities for target groups 1, 3 and 4 are carried out by a wide range of government units, in addition to the Ministry of Education. One of the very purposes of drawing up a national EFA plan is to integrate all EFA activities into a coherent concept and implementation framework. This will achieve better cost-efficiency, and greater impact on social and economic development than would be possible if they continued to be designed and carried out separately. Such coherent framework assigns clear roles to ECCD and NFE programmes. It sets priorities in terms of timing, specific populations groups, and allocation of public resources. The EFA plan must guide the activities of all actors, public and non-public alike. All EFA actors ought to conform their initiatives to the types of programmes and the priorities agreed in the ECCD and NFE parts of the EFA plan. This will make it possible for the government to ensure that many non-public actors adhere and conform to this framework.

When it comes to setting targets and priorities for resource allocation, the government has little choice: it must first serve the formal basic education subsector, at least its primary education component for which is committed by constitution or education law (or by the Dakar Framework for Action) to provide free formal education to all children of primary school age (or to all primary education pupils).

The fact that ECCD and preschool activities as well as NFE activities for out-of-school children and youth and adults are to a very large extent a matter of non-public initiatives and carried out by non-public organizations, makes the setting of realistic targets for ECCD and NFE particularly difficult. The targets set in the EFA plan are not legally or constitutionally binding for non-governmental (non-public, voluntary, private) organizations that are free to decide whether or not to allocate financial or other resources so that the EFA plan targets may be attained.

The non-public actors follow their own agenda, act once they have been able to mobilize resources and when they feel that conditions (i.e. the regulatory framework set by government) are adequate and propitious for their initiatives. Typically, ECCD and NFE activities are financed by the government only to the extent to which resources become available, i.e. have not been committed to formal basic education. Moreover, ECCD and NFE are competing for these resources with other education subsectors such as upper secondary, vocational and higher education.

Therefore, government planning for ECCD and NFE is more of a programmatic, indicative nature, setting out overall goals and objectives, and assessing overall resource implications. The aim is to provide a coherent framework within which the many non-governmental ECCD and NFE actors will be able to deploy their activities, rather than a detailed plan.

The chapters of the national EFA plan concerning ECCD and NFE indicate overall orders of magnitude and directions along which the Government will attempt to rally all actors, in particular non-governmental actors. The purpose of planning for ECCD and NFE is not the same as the purpose of planning for formal basic education.

While government planning for formal basic education (in countries where financing and service provision is mostly public) aims at guiding government decisions on resource allocations, government planning for NFE and ECCD aims at setting a coherent framework to orient and integrate activities undertaken by a wide range of public and non-public funding bodies and service providers.

This means that official Government EFA planning need not go through the trouble of formulating technically very detailed plans for ECCD and NFE. Instead of precise planning targets, the formulation of broad quantitative and qualitative national objectives and of broad programmes for ECCD and NFE development may suffice. The particular nature of ECCD and NFE makes it essential to organize the planning process in a participatory way, associating the large range of non-governmental funding bodies and service providers, to define jointly and create commitment towards the national objectives and priorities for ECCD and NFE.

Cost and Financing for EFA

The term "cost" has different meanings, depending on the context and the purpose for which it is used. In governmental education plans, such as EFA plans and plans for the development of basic education, the term "costs" designates the monetary value of all inputs required for the functioning of the education sector, as foreseen in the plan, and which must be provided for by the education authorities.

In the Basic Education sector the educational institutions (schools) are, as a rule, operated by government bodies (usually at community and district level). But there are also cases where basic education schools are operated by non-government, i.e. private bodies (in the legal form of associations, foundations, etc.). The costs for running the schools are paid out of the budgets of these bodies.

The costs of managing the sector, i.e. of all activities above the individual educational institutions, which include administration and pedagogical support, are usually borne by government units at higher levels (district, province, ministries). Government education plans contain only direct costs; i.e. the costs of goods and services required for the functioning of the educational institutions and for sector management, which are purchased with funds from the budgets of the authorities which operate the institutions. They include, for example, textbooks, other teaching and learning materials, premises, laboratory, library equipment, and salaries. It may happen that during plan implementation some items for which costs have been included in the plan will be provided in kind (e.g. services and materials for school construction provided without payment by members of the community). This reduces the funding needs, but it does not reduce costs, which must therefore be included in the plan.

Government education plans do not include indirect costs of education in the cost estimates and projections. Indirect costs are not paid from the budget of the institutions (or ministries), and therefore the plan makes no provision for their funding. Indirect costs include two types of costs:

(i) the monetary costs (i.e. expenditure) to parents for sending their children to school, including costs of clothing, food, transport, stationery, insurance, fees, user charges, etc.; and

(ii) costs to the families in the form of income foregone, because children attend school instead of earning revenue or helping their family to earn its living; and costs in the form of tax income foregone for the state because persons attend school instead of earning taxable revenue.

Assessing the indirect costs of education is nevertheless important for the formulation of the plan, since indirect costs are a decisive factor in determining the demand of families for education and in influencing the government's budget allocation pattern. Assessing indirect costs is therefore part. EFA Planning Guide of the sector analysis stage of planning, when information is gathered and analyzed for informed target setting for the plan. Costs of plan implementation which are financed from public sector budgets are called the public costs of education. Private costs of education have two components: (i) the costs of plan implementation that are not financed from public budgets, and (ii) the direct costs to parents of sending their children to school.

The two standardized categories of costs are capital costs and recurrent costs (or capital expenditure and recurrent expenditure). By law, they are standard in national accounts, national budgets, business accounting, and generally in accounting of all kinds of activities. They are also standard practice for estimating costs, preparing budgets and controlling expenditure of the education sector.

Usually, annual education sector budgets (and thus, annual plans) must be broken down by capital and recurrent expenditure. The costs of plans and budgets presented in the form of programmes must also be broken into capital and recurrent items, in addition to being presented in programme form.

Capital costs include items which occur only once, or from time to time, but not regularly every year, and not continuously; such as, infrastructure (construction) and expenditure the benefit of which lasts over a number of years (investments).

Recurrent costs include all items which occur regularly and continuously every year, which are used (consumed) the same year, and which cannot be used again next year. However, the distinction between recurrent and capital costs in education is not always clear-cut. For example, the production and distribution of textbooks is sometimes accounted as capital cost, and sometimes as recurrent cost. For the costing of the plan it is important to be consistent. Long-term and medium-term education plans are structured in the form of programmes, i.e. in groups of measures and activities corresponding directly to the same objective(s).

A programme usually comprises both capital and recurrent costs. There are different types of programmes. One type follows the structure of the education sector, designing programmes by sub-sector; i.e. a development programme for the preschool education subsector, another programme for the primary sub-sector, etc.. Another type of programme is oriented towards major functions, with a programme for quality improvement (which includes components such as teacher training, curriculum development, equipment, etc.), or a programme for access to education (which includes components such as school construction, school feeding, incentives for teachers, etc.).

Programme components can also be treated as programmes (e.g. teacher training, with the components of pre-service training and in-service training). For each programme, the costs have to be estimated for the plan period and for each budget year covered by the plan. In other words, the approach is that of programme planning and budgeting. An approach which has proven to be practical in costing a plan consists in grouping the planned activities into three functional programme categories:

— Cost category-1: Costs related to access to education (expanding access, in countries where the net enrolment rate is below 100%; and maintaining access in countries where universal enrollment is already attained);

— Cost category-2: Costs related to quality and relevance of education; and

— Cost category-3: Costs related to management of the education system..63 Cost and Financing Considerations These three functional categories of costs can be applied to any sub-sector or the education sector as a whole. They can also be applied for certain large components, e.g. teacher training, curriculum development, and decentralization.

Within these categories it is useful for purposes of analysis and projections to group the costs according to whether they are directly related, and therefore significantly sensitive to changes in the number of pupils, or teachers, or schools; or whether they are relatively insensitive.

For each cost category and each programme cost projections must be made for each plan-year and the entire plan period. There is no standardised way of making cost projections. A number of alternative approaches exist. An approach which has proven to be reliable and relatively simple consists of the following principal steps:

— *Projection Step 1*: determining the costs prevailing in the base year (the year preceding the first plan-year), by using standard unit costs, i.e. figures of average costs issued by the Ministry of Finance or the Government unit responsible for budget preparation. If such standard costs are not available, unit costs may be estimated based on the data contained in the most recent expenditure records for the relevant cost item. The use of standard unit costs makes cost estimates uniform, facilitates computations, ensures comparability, and allows checking and validating the estimates by different experts.

— *Projection Step-2:* projection of the development of each cost creating component of the plan, i.e. of the components of the education system. The principal components include: pupil enrolment, teachers, physical facilities, teaching/learning materials, activities aimed at ensuring quality and relevance of education, sector management. Each component may be broken down into a number of sub-components, for each of which projections are made.

— *Projection Step-3*: assessment of the resource implications of each of the projected components. For example: a projected enrolment increase implies an increase in the number of teachers, which in turn requires an increase of the total salary costs to be financed. Or, the introduction of a new curriculum implies special teacher training activities and special pedagogical support services, which in turn requires special funding.

— *Projection Step-4:* projection of the likely availability of funds. This takes into account (i) the share of the government budget likely to be allocated to the education sector, and (ii) the likely allocation of these funds within the education sector, i.e. between the different sub-sectors. The projections also assess the extent to which cost sharing is likely to yield funds for education. Making projections of financial resources likely to be available for the education sector is a complex task which should be undertaken by the Ministry of Planning and the Ministry of

Finance. Making.66 EFA Planning Guide projections for allocations within the sector is the task of the Ministry of Education, together with other education authorities at the provincial and district levels, and together with expertise from the Ministry of Planning and the Ministry of Finance. If resource allocation decisions are to attain the intended results they must be based on thorough insight into the functioning of the education sector.

— *Projection Step-5*: comparison of required resources with likely available resources. If there are resource gaps, three types of measures may be considered to close the gaps.

  — First: the cost components must be reviewed in order to identify possibilities of reducing the costs by improving the cost-efficiency of the resource utilisation. This includes changing targets (e.g. lowering the enrolment rate to be reached at the end of the plan period), and changing technical coefficients which determine the way in which the sector functions (e.g. increasing the pupil-teacher ratio).

  — Second: possibilities of increasing the funds must be explored. This includes more cost-sharing (e.g. by increasing user charges at secondary level, lowering subsidies to the provision of learning materials, etc.), and encouraging the creation of private education institutions, thereby reducing the financial burden on the government budget. Cost-sharing effects can also be simulated with the help of the EFA Analysis and Projection Model used for identifying possibilities of cost reductions. The sector analysis undertaken at the start of the planning process has already produced information and insights that provide clues for possible cost reductions.

— Third: the education authorities must lobby at appropriate government levels and negotiate a higher share of the national budget for the education sector.

All cost projections of the plan are expressed in actual prices of the base year, i.e. the year that precedes the first plan year. The figures for the first plan year are projections. The plan never includes projections of inflation. In other words, costs and finance projections are in real terms, not in current prices.The unit costs used for making cost projections are based on, and expressed in, base year prices. However, the value of certain unit costs does, in fact, increase during the plan period. This is typically the case of salaries, which increase every year, as a result of promotions and increments foreseen in the salary scale.

Adjustments for inflation will be made when annual budgets are prepared during the plan period. There are two ways of expressing these adjustments: (i) every year, the costs of the remaining plan period will be revised (upward) to take into account price increases that have occurred in the previous year, or (ii) the plan figures will not change; instead, the annual budget will take into account the price increases which have occurred since the beginning of the plan.

Financing plan

The education plan is not credible unless it shows how the required expenditure can be financed. This can best be done by including at least outline financing plans for the programmes in the plan.

The programmes of the education plan are part of the overall national development efforts. For allocation of financial resources, they compete with all the other sectors such as health, agriculture, transport, etc.. The resources needed by the education sector (including the resources for EFA plan implementation) will have to be considered along with claims of other sectors of the economy, as expressed in the plans of other ministries and in the national development plan. In preparing the education sector plan, planners have to be careful to propose programmes set within reasonable limits of resource requirements if they are to stand a chance of being implemented.

One way of making planning assumptions on resource ceilings for the education sector is to assume that the minimum ceiling in the future is the present share of the education sector in the national budget. However, in a situation where the education policy goals for the plan period imply an increase of the education sector share, planners must seek to convince the providers of resources to change the resource allocation pattern in favour of education.

Reliable indications of likely available resource levels are at the disposal of the plan preparation team early in the plan preparation process. The planning team needs indications concerning the share of the sector budget in the total government budget, and/or growth rates of the share, or of major cost items (such as salaries, materials, etc.). Indications of likely resource levels have to be provided by the Ministry of Planning and the Ministry of Finance.

In most countries it is difficult for the Education Minister to obtain, early in the planning process, reliable indications on levels of resource availability, because Planning and Finance Ministries are waiting to first see the education plan. But without at least some preliminary indications of resource levels, the education plan cannot be drawn up. This difficulty can be overcome through a continuous, iterative process of putting forward, by the education planners, preliminary programme proposals and related resource requirements, and of revising them in the light of arguments, considerations and facts brought forward by the providers of resources.

A good way of conducting such an iterative process is to closely associate the Ministries of Planning and Finance to the education plan preparation work from the very beginning, and to create and maintain close and continuous dialogue. In this way, there is a good chance that the decision levels in the Planning and Finance Ministries will gain sufficient insight into the functioning of the education sector, and a better understanding of the programmes included in the education plan as well as of the reasonableness of the resource requirements of the education sector.

Bibliography

Apps, Jerold., *Leadership for the Emerging Age: Transforming Practice in Adult and Continuing Education*. Jossey-Bass Publishers., 1994.

Bhola, H., "Literature on Adult Literacy: New Directions in the 1980's" *Comparative Education Review*, 34 (2), 1990.

Bock, J. C., and G. J. *Papagiannis, Nonformal Education and National Development: A Critical Assessment of Policy, Research, and Practice*. New York: Praeger, 1983.

Brizius, J.A., & S.A. Foster, *Generation to generation: Realizing the promise of family literacy*, The National Center for Family Literacy. Michigan: High/Scope Press, 1993.

C.K. Pathak, *Adult Education : Millennium Challenges*, New Delhi, Rajat Pub., 2003.

Clark, M. Tennessee, *Meeting the needs of the adult learner: using nonformal education for social action*, Highlander Popular Education Center, 1978.

Hoxeng, James, *Let Jorge do it: An approach to rural nonformal education*. Amherst, MA: University of Massachusetts, Center for International Education, 1973.

Inkeles, A., *Education and Individual Modernity in Developing Countries*. Leiden: E. J. Brill, 1974.

Jagannath Mohanty. *Adult and Non-Formal Education*, New Delhi, Deep & Deep, 2002.

K. Venkata Reddy, *Changing Attitudes to Education in India*, New Delhi, Atlantic Pub., 2002.

Kindervatter, S., *Nonformal Education as an Empowering Process.* Amherst, MA: Center for International Education, 1979.

Marmar Mukhopadhyay, *Education for a Global Society : Inter-faith Dimensions*, Delhi, Shipra, 2003.

R.B.L. Soni, *Attitudes Towards Integrated Education*, New Delhi, Rajat, 2001.

Renu Nanda, *Non-Formal Education at Cross-Roads/Concepts, Responses, Strategies and Findings*, Jammu, Vinod Pub., 2003.

S. Venkataiah, (ed.), *Non-Formal Education*, New Delhi, Anmol, 2001.

S.C. Joshi, (ed.), *Dynamics of Non-Formal Education*, new Delhi, Akansha, 2002

S.P. Agrawal, Mithilesh Gupta, M.W.K. Sherwani and Meena Usmani, *Development of Adult, Continuing and Non-Formal Education in India*, New Delhi, Concept, 2002.

Index